The Legacy of
Abraham Kuyper

The Legacy of
Abraham Kuyper

by Harry Van Dyke

PUBLISHING
εν αρχη ην ο λογος
AALTEN, THE NETHERLANDS

WORDBRIDGE PUBLISHING
Aalten, the Netherlands
www.wordbridge.net
info@wordbridge.net

Copyright © 2024 Harry Van Dyke.

ISBN 978–90–76660–76–9 paperback
       978–90–76660–77–6 hardback

All rights reserved. This book or any portion thereof may not be reproduced or used in any manner whatsoever without the express written permission of the copyright holder except for the use of brief quotations.

ILLUSTRATION: Abraham Kuyper as a young MP (1874-1876). Photographic reproduction courtesy Wikimedia Commons. This reproduction is in the public domain.

TABLE OF CONTENTS

Preface vii
   Plan of the Book... viii
   Sources viii
I. Kuyper as Heir... 1
   Willem Bilderdijk (1756–1831): framing a worldview 1
   Isaac da Costa (1798–1860): challenging the spirit of the age............ 7
   G. Groen van Prinsterer (1801–1876): principle vs. principle 10
   Otto Gerhard Heldring (1804–1876): calling for united action 19
   Johan Adam Wormser (1807–1862): abandoning
      establishmentarianism 21
   Isaac Esser (1818–1885): educating the common people 24
   Klaas Kater (1850–1916): mobilizing the working classes 27
   Abraham Kuyper (1837–1920): seizing the initiative 39
   Summary... 47
II. Kuyper's Heirs.. 49
   L. W. Chr. Keuchenius (1822–1893): formulating an ethical
      colonial policy.. 50
   Alexander Idenburg (1861–1935): christianizing the public ethos. 53
   Syb Talma (1864–1916): democracy under the rule of Christ........ 57
   Alexander Frederik de Savornin Lohman (1837–1924): true
      educational pluralism.. 63
   Jan Schouten (1883–1963): discerning the revolution in modern
      dress.. 64
   Victor Henri Rutgers (1877–1945): confronting the modern
      dictator 66
   Herman Dooyeweerd (1894–1977): a new critique of theoretical
      thought.. 69
   Summary... 73
III. Some Lessons from This History... 75
IV. Some Protestant Pillars... 81
Index of Names 87
Index of Subjects 89

PREFACE

Like any legacy, a cultural legacy cuts both ways: it can be the legacy left behind by those who came before you, and the legacy you leave behind for those who come after you. Both kinds are included when we think of "the legacy of Abraham Kuyper."

You might be forgiven for forgetting this double legacy if you attended the commemoration of Kuyper's *Stone Lectures on Calvinism* at Princeton in February, 1998.[1] The featured speakers created the impression that once upon a time there lived a historical figure by the name of Abraham Kuyper, a Dutch scholar and perhaps also a politician who a century ago had been a blazing comet that for a time lit up the sky over his little country and then disappeared beyond the horizon, a dynamic person who came from nowhere and then seemed to have vanished without a trace.

Of course, we all knew better. Yet no one so much as mentioned that Kuyper had many forerunners and even more followers. My aim with this little book is twofold. I would like us to explore Kuyper's legacy in both senses.

───────────────

[1] The event commemorated the 100th anniversary of Kuyper's Stone Lectures. When the organizers announced the event some months in advance, they expected that perhaps 40 people would register. To their surprise, 400 signed up, including a busload of college students accompanied by their professor and about twenty staff members of the Christian Labour Association of Canada.

Plan of the Book

First, I want to show that Kuyper rejuvenated Dutch Calvinism—brought it "into rapport with the times," as he used to put it, inviting the name Neo-Calvinism. He was able to achieve this by building on a movement that was nearly a hundred years old, a legacy of which he became the grateful heir. Part I deals with that neglected topic. Each of Kuyper's forerunners made a unique contribution to the tradition that he inherited and turned to political profit. Brief sketches about each of seven forerunners—namely, Bilderdijk, Da Costa, Groen van Prinsterer, Heldring, Wormser, Esser, and Kater—may be helpful in explaining the impact that Kuyper had in his own day.

Secondly, I wish to highlight a select few of Kuyper's many followers who in turn built on his legacy and so became his heirs. Part II contains a brief account of historic contributions made by seven of Kuyper's heirs—namely, Keuchenius, Idenburg, Lohman, Talma, Schouten, Rutgers, and Dooyeweerd.

Part III, finally, draws some lessons from all this history, while Part IV describes one instance of the peculiar phenomenon of "pillarization."

Sources

Part I, "Kuyper as Heir," is a slightly revised version of a paper presented at the international conference "Christianity and Culture: The Heritage of Abraham Kuyper on Different Continents," held at the Free University in Amsterdam on 9–11 June 1998. The paper was published in the volume *On Kuyper: A Collection of Readings on the Life, Work and Legacy of Abraham Kuyper*, edited by Steve Bishop and John H. Kok (Sioux

Preface

Centre, IA: Dordt College Press, 2013), 7–26. Select portions were also used as a contribution to a festschrift for Professor John C. VanderStelt entitled *Marginal Resistance* (Dordt College Press, 2001), 1–23. Some more recent literature has now been added in the footnotes.

Parts II and III, "Kuyper's Heirs" and "Some Lessons from this History," are the texts, not published earlier, of a contribution to a "missiological consultation" with Lesslie Newbiggin (1909–1998) on the theme of "Kuyperianism and the Public Square: A Tradition of Christian Cultural Engagement." This event was held in Leeds, UK, 18–21 June 1996, in the conference centre of the West Yorkshire School of Christian Studies attached to the home of Dr. David Hanson. The "consultation" was organized by Drs. Michael Goheen and George VanderVelde at Newbiggin's request after their discussions with him had aroused his curiosity about the Dutch experiment in "Christian cultural engagement."

The text of Part IV was distributed at the consultation mentioned above.

Hamilton, Ontario　　　　　　　　　　Harry Van Dyke, D. Litt.
Spring 2024　　　　　　　　　　　　　　Redeemer University

I. KUYPER AS HEIR

The tradition of Neo-Calvinism to which we attach the name of Abraham Kuyper (and, not to forget, Herman Bavinck) went through its birth pangs toward the end of the eighteenth century. A spirit of confronting and countering secular modernity began to stir in the Netherlands in writers like Hieronymus van Alphen (1746–1803) and Willem Bilderdijk (1756–1831). Van Alphen was a civil servant and a poet, who in 1801 published his "tract for the times" entitled *Preach the Gospel to Every Creature*. More importantly, his contemporary Bilderdijk, a barrister and a poet, developed into a major figure in the Christian Counter-Enlightenment.

Willem Bilderdijk (1756–1831): framing a worldview

Born in the same year as Mozart and dying in the same year as Hegel, Bilderdijk was not only a literary artist but also a historian. Straddling the 18th and 19th centuries, he was an incorrigible Romantic who resisted the Enlightenment both philosophically and politically. In 1795, when French and Patriot armies inundated his country and installed a Revolutionary regime, this practicing lawyer refused to swear the new oath of allegiance and was forced into exile. During the Restoration the now old man earned a modest living as a private lecturer in Leyden. He attracted students of some of the better families in the land, "corrupting the flower of our youth" (as one observer noted with alarm) by bitter invectives against the spirit of the age and blistering attacks on the "received opinions" of the ruling elite. He delivered himself of his high-flying harangues harum-scarum, in a dazzling display of astonishing erudition. In this brusque way Bilderdijk broke the monopoly of the Regent interpretation of Dutch history, a version which (not unlike British Whiggism) attributed the growth of liberty to the republican forefathers of the ruling middle classes, in disregard of the role of the Reformed "little people" and the House of Orange. Thirteen volumes of his *History of the Fatherland* were published posthumously, as were 16 volumes of his *Collected Poems*.

One of those poems captures a core idea of the tradition we are tracing. In his sonnet *De Wareld* (1786), Bilderdijk passes in review the great schools of philosophy throughout Western history to find an answer to one of the most fundamental questions mankind can pose: *What is the world?* Can we unlock its secret and know it in its deepest essence? Here is my approximation of that poem:

The World

What are you, structured frame 'yond mental powers' clasp?
    Chain of effect from cause, to which there is no end,
    Whose possibility the mind can't comprehend,
Whose actuality our reason fails to grasp?
O deep abyss, where can our consciousness then enter?
    What are you? Mere appearance, pressed upon the sense?
    An imprint of the mind, remaining ever dense?
A notion that we forge, like a conceited mentor?
    Or is your being then external to, though near me?
    Do you exist? Is not existence just illusion?

I. Kuyper as Heir

> Or of some other being but a mere effusion?
> Thus did I fret myself, until God answered: Hear Me!
> All things depend on me; whatever is, is mine:
> The whole world is my voice and summons you to fear me.

In the first quatrain the poet wonders whether the mystery of the universe will yield to human understanding. Line 2: Is the world a universal concatenation of causes—as the Stoics taught? Lines 3 and 4: This the mind can hardly conceive: the world just is—but don't ask how.

The second quatrain gives voice to modern philosophers. Line 6: Is the world mere sense perception—as British empiricism held? Lines 7 and 8: Or a mental impression only, a concept, an idea—as maintained in German idealism?

And so the octet proceeds: from ancient philosophical skepticism to modern philosophical subjectivism which grounds reality in the creative powers of the human mind.[2]

The journey thus far has not laid the poet's quest to rest. Other schools of thought will now be consulted. This marks the turn in the sestet of the sonnet. Line 9: In the Middle Ages solipsism was avoided by affirming the reality of substance, with objective existence outside of oneself. Line 10: But perhaps "existence" is no more than an illusion? Line 11: Or perhaps an emanation from a higher Being—as Neoplatonists believed?

The poet finds no rest in any of these answers. His survey of philosophy has only wearied him. So he goes straight to the

---

[2] I am relying on an undated offprint of a perceptive analysis by D. F. M. Strauss in the journal *Roeping en Riglyne*.

source of all Wisdom. Here, at line 12, is the real turn in the sonnet: God himself instructs him how to understand the world: The world is a word, and it says: The world belongs to God. Fear God and keep his commandments, for this is the whole duty of man. That is the conclusion of the matter.

What might be the significance of this poem? According to Bilderdijk scholar Jan Bosch, this sonnet contains the poet's worldview in a nutshell: "the calling voice of God that resonates in the human heart."[3] Even more importantly, as Bosch also notes, the sonnet marks the "first attempt in Dutch at a Christian totalizing thought oriented to the true Origin of the cosmos."[4] Herman Bavinck has remarked that for Bilderdijk everything that is, is an image or analogy "pointing to a spiritual world which lies behind it and which reveals something of the virtues and perfections of God"; the creature has no existence in and of itself, and must be given its being from moment to moment by the Creator.[5]

To return to the sonnet, its significance surely lies in being an attempt at framing a comprehensive approach to the burden of philosophy, an approach that proceeds unequivocally from the Christian concept of creation and resolutely renounces all notions of the self-sufficiency of the world and of human autonomy: whatever is, depends on God, and is ori-

---

[3] J. Bosch, "Willem Bilderdijk als wijsgerig historievormer," in *Perspectief; feestbundel van de jongeren bij het 25-jarig bestaan van de Vereniging voor Calvinistische Wijsbegeerte* (Kampen: Kok, 1961), pp. 228–240, at p. 233.

[4] Ibid., p. 229.

[5] H. Bavinck, *Bilderdijk als denker en dichter* (Kampen: Kok, 1906), 56.

ented toward Him in a perpetually restless mode of being. Particularly appealing is the poet's unabashed confessional stance with which he enters, as it were, a philosophical "dialogue," a stance that is intensely relevant and apropos to this dialogue, not shutting down the discussion with a theological dictum but pinpointing the essence of each successive philosophical school. After his immersion in centuries of metaphysical speculation, Bilderdijk emerges to the surface and reaches directly for a profoundly religious response.

To be sure, we know from history that the personal life of the poet was compromised, yet not his life-principle. As well, the question has been raised—in the splendid intellectual biography that came out recently—whether the sonnet is a true reflection of the poet's own conception at that moment in time.[6] That is an intriguing question, but not germane to our inquiry here. What the published sonnet did in those years was to adjure contemporaries to resist the temptation to compromise with worldly patterns of thought; it encouraged them not to be timid in the face of the canon of Western philosophy—not to hesitate about the perfect right of Revelation to instruct Reason. It would be anachronistic to call Bilderdijk a *Neo*-Calvinist, yet he foreshadows a basic conviction of Neo-Calvinism, namely (to quote a recent study of the movement)

---

[6] Joris van Eijnatten, *Hogere sferen: de ideeënwereld van Willem Bilderdijk* (Hilversum: Verloren, 1998), 84.

that "Christianity can challenge, subvert and fulfill the cultures and philosophical systems of every age."[7]

Bilderdijk's answer foreshadows Kuyper's emphasis on taking creation and man's calling in it as one's starting point also for thought. True, Kuyper may have claimed a bit too much in his commemoration address on the sesquicentennial of Bilderdijk's birth,[8] but he was correct in recognizing Bilderdijk as a man of importance not only for the Dutch nation but also for the Calvinist revival of the 19th century. Bilderdijk wrote many tracts in defence of the faith of the Reformation, heaping scorn upon its modern detractors. We might not want to go so far as to assert with the author of a popular biography that Bilderdijk carried the old-time religion single-handedly, Noah-like, from the old world of its near total eclipse into the new world of the 19th century where it would flourish once more.[9] Nevertheless, one can only be grateful for Bilderdijk's historical significance as a preserving force in a destructive age. The age was throttling the faith of the Reformation, but Bilderdijk's pen was an instrument that helped keep it alive. In effect, he inaugurated a tradition that would be both aggressive in confronting modern culture and comprehensive in positing its counterclaims.

---

[7] N. Gray Sutanto and Cory C. Brock, *Neo-Calvinism; A Theological Introduction* (Bellingham, WA: Lexham, 2022), p. 293, Thesis 2.

[8] A. Kuyper, *Bilderdijk in zijne nationale beteekenis; rede gehouden te Amsterdam op 1 Oct. 1906* (Amsterdam and Pretoria: Höveker & Wormser, 1906).

[9] Rudolf van Reest, *'n Onbegrieplijk mensch; het leven van Mr W. Bilderdijk*, 2nd impr. (Goes: Oosterbaan & Le Cointre, 1940), 259, 270–271.

Isaac da Costa (1798–1860): challenging the spirit of the age

It was another poet[10] who first gave voice to a key strategy of the Kuyperian tradition. The story of this Sephardic Jew from Amsterdam begins with his conversion (and that of his cousin and bosom friend Abraham Capadose) around 1818 in Leyden, where both were studying law. The two friends would be lifelong adherents of the Réveil in the Netherlands, a movement that kindled evangelical fervour well beyond the middle of the century. The Dutch Réveil was a revival of Christian faith and the Christian life, an amalgam of an indigenous revived Calvinism (such as represented by Bilderdijk) and important influences from abroad (notably from Switzerland). The Réveil became the nursery of resistance to the dechristianization of Dutch society. Ultimately it was to put Reformed people back in the centre of public life. Its aim was to re-Christianize modern culture using modern means, under the motto, "faith working by love."

The birth-cry of the Dutch awakening is generally held to have been Isaac da Costa's notorious broadside of 1823, *Grievances Against the Spirit of the Age*. In rather intemperate language the tract fulminated against the shallow optimism of the time and derided the complacent beliefs in social progress and human perfectibility. It was a declaration of war on the Enlightenment project as this was beginning to make headway in the Netherlands—a pointed repudiation of that project's

---

[10] See Isaac da Costa, *Kompleete Dichtwerken*, ed. Hasebroek, 3 vols., 8th impr. (Leyden: Sijthoff, n.d.).

basic premise: human autonomy, the banning of Christian principles from the seats of learning and from the public arena.

Public opinion was so scandalized by the pamphlet that its author's home for a time was given police protection because of threats. The aging Bilderdijk came to the defence of his pupil, but this only added to the ire of liberal newspapers such as the Arnhem Courant, which lampooned Da Costa as "the conceited monkey of the old baboon."[11] Eventually Da Costa saw himself compelled to abandon his legal practice and spend the rest of his days as a man of letters, as a lecturer (by subscription) on historical and religious subjects, and as the host of Sunday soirées where he led in Bible study, framed by much prayer and song.[12]

By mid-century Isaac da Costa had developed into a forward-looking Christian citizen. He espoused the need to update the tools of orthodox Christians in order to help them stay abreast of their times, not just for self-preservation but also for being a more effective witness. Scientific theology would have to be taken vigorously in hand, followed by developing a progressive political program in which the eternal principles of the Word of God would be applied to the problems of the day. The Revolution of 1795, and again of 1848, while evil in themselves, had nevertheless introduced fresh ways and means, such as participatory government and

---

[11] Cf. D. J. A. Westerhuis, "De 'Arnhemsche Courant' contra Da Costa ultimo anno 1823," *Stemmen des Tijds* 14.3 (1925): 370–377.

[12] See Gerrit J. ten Zythoff, *Sources of Secession: The Netherlands Hervormde Kerk on the Eve of the Dutch Immigration to the Midwest* (Grand Rapids, MI.: Eerdmans, 1987), 57–97; cf. M. E. Kluit, *Het Protestantse Réveil in Nederland en daarbuiten, 1815–1865* (Amsterdam, 1974), 167.

disestablishment, that could serve as providential tools of which Christians should avail themselves to contribute to the "unfolding of God's counsel for mankind." We are to be *against* our age, but also *of* our age, he wrote to his friend Groen van Prinsterer.[13] The year before, Da Costa had been instrumental in organizing a voters' association in his riding in Amsterdam and writing a program for it—"in its essence, a fruit of *the* ages; in its form, of *this* age!"—or as he would put it in another one of his occasional poems: We will not be led by the spirit of the age and its errant light, yet we shall always distinguish the *spirit* of the age from the *course* of the age.[14] There was much common sense in Da Costa's cultural strategy:

> The malady of our age must be combated with the means which, by God's all-wise providence, are given in the malady itself ... No abolition of written constitutions, no formal restoration of a Calvinist state and church can give us back the historical and truly spiritual principle.... The adversary must be conquered, at any rate combated, on his own terrain ...[15]

---

[13] Da Costa to Groen, 18 July 1852; in *Brieven van Mr. Isaac da Costa*, ed. G. Groen van Prinsterer (Amsterdam, 1873), 2:91–93.

[14] Isaac da Costa, *Kompleete Dichtwerken*, ed. Hasebroek, 3 vols., 8th impr. (Leyden: Sijthoff, n.d.), 2:253, 3:121.

[15] Da Costa to Groen, 11 Nov. 1852; in *Brieven van Mr. Isaac da Costa*, 2:105–106. Cf. J. C. Rullmann, "Da Costa in zijn beteekenis voor de anti-revolutionaire partij," *Anti-Revolutionaire Staatkunde* 2 (1926): 165–188, 225–244; J. C. Rullmann, "Het Réveil en de opkomst der Anti-Revolutionaire Partij," *Anti-Revolutionaire Staatkunde* 4 (1928): 461–476.

This directive foreshadowed the realignment of cultural forces that began to show its initial contours in the 1850s under the leadership of Groen van Prinsterer. "Combating the adversary on his own terrain" became the battle-cry for all who would march in this tradition.

G. Groen van Prinsterer (1801–1876): principle vs. principle

Like Da Costa, Groen van Prinsterer early determined that he had to be in fundamental ("principial") opposition to the whole tenor of his age. Attendance at Bilderdijk's private lectures during his student years at Leyden first sowed the seeds of this nonconformism. Such a stance might have condemned Willem Groen (as he was known) to a lifetime of sterile reaction, were it not for his belief that a third way was possible, a path between revolution and counter-revolution, an approach to problems that would be *anti-revolutionary*— that is, opposed to the "systematic overturning of ideas" whereby truth and justice are founded on human opinion rather than divine ordinance—and simultaneously an approach that would be *Christian-historical*—that is, open to revealed norms for human life, corroborated by the experience of the ages.

Like Edmund Burke, Groen appreciated history as "the known march of the ordinary providence of God." While the Scriptures always had priority for him, he felt it was neither prudent nor godly to fly in the face of past wisdom, particularly where it reflected biblical maxims and gospel mandates.

It was very much Groen's trenchant analysis of the nature of modernity that determined the strategy for a century of distinctive Christian action in his country. Groen formed a

I. Kuyper as Heir

bridge between the spontaneous early protestors against theological liberalism and the secularization of politics, such as Bilderdijk and Da Costa, and the systematic antirevolutionary theorists that would come after him, such as Kuyper and Dooyeweerd. In his lecture series of 1845–46, published the following year under the title *Ongeloof en Revolutie*,[16] Groen threw down the gauntlet against the leading lights of his day. The root cause of the malaise of the age, he set forth, was unbelief—unbelief, or apostasy, as it was first elaborated into a system and then applied in a gigantic social experiment. It was the Enlightenment that had dismissed God's Word as revealed truth and Christian traditions as the basis of society, replacing them with a twofold "philosophy of unbelief," one that recognized no truth beyond human reason and no authority apart from human consent. The lectures traced the outworking of this new philosophy: the supremacy of reason produces atheism in religion and materialism in morality, while the supremacy of the human will leads to popular sovereignty in political theory and anarchy in political practice. These logical outcomes had been dramatically revealed in the French Revolution and in all subsequent emulations of that great experiment.

According to Groen, therefore, a correct appraisal of the French Revolution and its aftermath must take into account its profoundly religious impulse. By religion he meant man's ultimate commitment, either to God or to whatever takes

---

[16] For an abridged translation, see Guillaume Groen van Prinsterer, *Unbelief and Revolution*, ed. and trans. Harry Van Dyke (Bellingham, WA: Lexham Press, 2018).

God's place. Religion thus defined had been the motor of the events that launched the modern world; the Revolution of 1789 was driven by a surrogate religion, namely the ideology of secular liberalism. This ideology was not renounced in the Restoration of 1815. Consequently, the same subversive ideas continued to undermine the foundations of society and to stifle wholesome reform. Eventually, Groen predicted, these ideas would ignite fresh flare-ups of revolutionary violence. Like Tocqueville, he came to the disturbing conclusion that the Revolution had become a permanent feature of European civilization. "Only from a revival of Christian charity and Evangelical spirit," he wrote, "can we draw the strength to match unbelief. Only through faith in the Son of the living God can the Revolution be vanquished."[17] We are living in a condition of permanent revolution, so ended his lectures; revolutions are here to stay and will grow in scope and intensity—unless men can be persuaded to return to the Christian religion and practice the Gospel and its precepts in their full implications for human life and civilized society. Barring such a revival, the future would belong to the most consistent sects of the new secular religion, socialism and communism.[18]

In Groen's estimation, the political spectrum that presented itself to his generation offered no meaningful

---

[17] Ibid., 221.

[18] A perceptive British reaction to Groen's book appeared after some portions of it had been translated and published in English: at the Westminster Conference of 1975, D. Martyn Lloyd-Jones addressed the audience on the topic of "The French Revolution and After," quoting copiously from Lecture XI of *Unbelief and Revolution*. See *The Christian and the State in Revolutionary Times* (London, 1975), 94–99.

I. Kuyper as Heir

choice. The radical left was composed of fanatical believers in the "theory of practical atheism"; the liberal centre was occupied by warm sympathizers who nevertheless cautioned against excesses and preached moderation in living out the new creed; the conservative right included all who lacked either the wit, the wisdom, or the will to repudiate the modern tenets yet who recoiled from the consequences whenever the ideology was implemented in any consistent way. Thus, none of the three "nuances" of secular liberalism represented a valid option for Christian citizens. Groen ended his lectures with a compelling invitation to resist "the Revolution" in whatever form it manifested itself and to work for radical alternatives in politics, along *anti*-revolutionary, Christian-historical lines. "Resist beginnings" and "Principle over against principle" became the watchwords of the Anti-revolution. Groen's radicalism would later be expressed by Abraham Kuyper in words that capture the gist of the Neo-Calvinist movement that he mobilized into a fighting force:

> If the battle is to be fought with honor and with a hope of victory, then principle must be arrayed against principle; then it must be felt that in Modernism the vast energy of an all-embracing life-system assails us; then also it must be understood that we have to take our stand in a life-system of equally comprehensive and far-reaching power.[19]

---

[19] A. Kuyper, *Lectures on Calvinism* (Grand Rapids, MI: Eerdmans, 1931), 20.

When the book *Unbelief and Revolution* came out and its author sent complimentary copies to his friends, their reactions were telling. Aeneas baron Mackay wrote to Groen: "The Word applied to politics was new to me, and now that I have placed that candle in the darkness I see sorry things, but I see."[20]

Elout van Soeterwoude felled compelled to question the implied vision of a Christian state and a Christian society. Would positing an alternative "principle" suffice to bring that about? And had so-called "anti-revolutionary forms" ever been more than just Ideal-types, he wondered. "I have always believed," he submitted,

> that wherever men feared God they strove after such forms; wherever the Christian religion has lived in men's hearts since the Reformation, such forms have been realized here and there, yet always but in part, and the more these things weakened and vanished, the more did men depart from them and did the revolutionary spirit gain ascendancy. It was therefore always the good that a few people desired and accomplished—in faith, in the fear and power of God. But it was hardly the principle of the State. Nor will it ever be.[21]

Elout's caution would never be forgotten as the tradition grew in strength. The goal would not be a repristination of a Constantinian link between Church and State. At the same

---

[20] Mackay to Groen, 26 Aug. 1847; in G. Groen van Prinsterer, *Schriftelijke Nalatenschap. Briefwisseling*, ed. J. L. van Essen et al., 6 vols. (The Hague: Nijhoff, 1949–1992), III, 810.

[21] Elout to Groen, 23 June 1849; in *Briefwisseling*, III, 27.

I. Kuyper as Heir

time, a love of church and nation would encourage anti-revolutionaries not to flag in their zeal to provide Christian leadership for state and society. For Elout continued:

> Yet anywhere, at any time, even today, God can raise up leaders who administer affairs for a time in a Christian spirit. Apart from Christ, the principle, even if accepted, is dead. Will the majority ever be Christian? I think not; but [it may] perhaps submit for a time to the power of faith. Hence your labour is not in vain.[22]

Groen's acquaintance, the poet-theologian Nicolaas Beets, wrote to tell him that he had found the book gripping:

> I could not put it down until I had read it all and yesterday afternoon closed the book with a prayer on my lips.... Your book makes it clear to me: the nations are walking in ways where no return is likely, no halt avails, and progress is the increasing manifestation of the man of sin. Who can arrest, who can deliver but the Lord alone?[23]

Beets's younger colleague J. P. Hasebroek wrote to the author that *Unbelief and Revolution* had greatly clarified for him the relation between gospel and politics. To be sure, he had always believed that the Word of God, as absolute truth, contained the core of all truths, including the basic principles of all genuine political science; but Groen's book provided a

---

[22] Ibid., 28.
[23] Beets to Groen, 8 Sept. 1847; in *Briefwisseling*, II, 812.

yardstick by which "all the new phenomena emerging in the politics and society of our time may be measured and evaluated."[24]

When the book was reissued twenty years later, Professor De Geer of Utrecht made a telling remark. "Unbelief is showing itself more brazen every day," he observed, adding a concern which was Groen's concern exactly: What are the faithful doing about it? They have no sense of what it means to be church. Christian action, he complained, is paralyzed by internal division and individualism. Unbelief can do what it wants: it finds itself opposed by isolated individuals only.[25]

It would be another four years after this lament before Kuyper would raise his *Standaard* to overcome this individualism by means of a Groenian type of "isolationism": that is, *to rally* the Christian body for developing a collective Christian political mind, and then on that basis *to orchestrate* united Christian action. That mobilization was possible after 1872 because of Groen's lifelong "strategy" of retrenchment: namely, to identify the non-negotiables and stand by one's principles. "In our isolation lies our strength," he insisted to the (at first tiny) party of his followers, explaining: We do not mean thereby that we want to be "political hermits" but that we have a "distinctive point of departure." To establish and preserve one's distinctiveness would keep one's identity intact and one's testimony pure: "I would rather end up in the company of

---

[24] Hasebroek to Groen, 22 Sept. 1847; in *Briefwisseling*, II, 820f; see also III, 851.

[25] De Geer to Groen, 11 Oct. 1868; in *Briefwisseling*, IV, 261. Cf. Groen, *Unbelief and Revolution*, 236–248: "a word about the calling of those who confess the Gospel..."

only a few or, if necessary, all alone, than abandon a starting point without which we would not only lose our influence but cease being a party."[26] This kind of uncompromising radicalism goes far in explaining the stamina and perseverance that this tradition exhibited in years to come as it faced perennial opposition and personal defeats. At bottom it was rooted in choosing faithful obedience over worldly success.

Much of Groen's moral support came from the silent majority in the land whom he referred to as "the people behind the voters." He meant that portion of the population who held to the Reformed faith but who had no voting rights because they lacked the property or income qualifications and thus paid little or no taxes. Groen took comfort and courage from the knowledge that they daily held him up in prayer. It irked the opposition to hear Groen claim in the lower house of Parliament that he did not just represent a fraction of the population but the "core of the nation." The party of the "anti-Revolution" was pre-eminently a "national party," Groen insisted, not only because it is linked "to the faith of our fathers and our historical traditions" but also because its program "resonates in the Christian conscience of the Dutch people." At the end of his life Groen noted with gratitude that "as long as I was faithful [in politics and public affairs], the orthodox people were never unfaithful to me."[27]

---

[26] G. Groen van Prinsterer, *Parlementaire Studiën en Schetsen*, 3 vols. (The Hague, 1866), II, 336–337.

[27] Quoted in H. Smitskamp, *Wat heeft Groen van Prinsterer ons vandaag te zeggen?* (The Hague: Daamen, 1945), 28; see also 118, 124–128.

Central to Groen's career was his defence of freedom of education. He called it "freedom of religion with respect to one's children." [28] In parliament and in the press, he spearheaded the campaign against the common or comprehensive, religiously mixed government schools for primary education. At first, he and his friends fought for the mere right as private citizens to establish alternative schools, a right that was at first denied by the local authorities, members of the ruling elite. When this right was at last recognized, following some years after a Royal Decree had been issued to that effect, a movement for explicitly Christian schools began to take root throughout the country, and Groen now condemned the practice of restricting public funding to government schools. He denied the possibility of religious neutrality in education. In his estimation, modernists were using public education in the hope of transcending religious differences through a strictly rational approach and preparing children to become right-thinking adults in a unified secular society. In practice, the so-called neutrality of the government school, Groen observed in 1861, "grows into the most pernicious partiality favouring unbelief and ends in making proselytes for the religion of reason and nature."[29]

The schools struggle, which did not end until the pacification bill of 1920, was Groen's most important legacy to his

---

[28] G. Groen van Prinsterer, *Bijdrage tot herziening der Grondwet in Nederlandsche zin* (Leyden, 1840), 89.

[29] G. Groen van Prinsterer, "Kosteloosheid van het Openbaar Onderwijs en Christendom boven Geloofsverdeeldheid" [Tuition-free public education and Christianity above sectarianism], in *Bijdragen der Vereeniging voor Christelijk-Nationaal Schoolonderwijs* (The Hague, 1861), appendix.

nation, a nation that escaped a monolithic society based on secular liberalism only when liberals at last were forced to concede that in education there ought to be equal rights or a level playing field for all citizens. It was the schools struggle that would first put Abraham Kuyper onto the national stage.

Otto Gerhard Heldring (1804–1876): calling for united action

This country pastor was to give the initial impulse for united Christian action in his country. His parish work had brought him face to face with the wretched conditions of peasants and day-labourers. Inspired by Ezekiel 34:4,[30] he became involved in land reclamation, the digging of wells, and literacy programs through conducting night classes and composing readers for the young. He pioneered the establishment of homes for orphans and for neglected children.[31] Since all this cost a great deal of money, Heldring became a master beggar, via letters and visits in *Réveil* circles, to raise funds for his many philanthropic causes. When the Society for the Utility of the Commonweal, active in promoting public education nationwide, approached him with a lucrative offer for adopting one of his readers, on condition that he suppress certain passages

---

[30] "The weak you have not strengthened, the sick you have not healed, the injured you have not bound up, the strayed you not brought back, the lost you have not sought, and with force and harshness you have ruled them" (ESV).

[31] See John de Liefde's articles on "Pastor Heldring" in *The Christian Miscellany and Family Visitor* (1856), 240–243, 272–274; *The British Messenger* (April 1863), 40ff; and *The Sunday Magazine* (Feb. 1865), 321–325.

deemed "too sectarian," the pious author was briefly tempted, he confessed to his friends, to compromise, but he had ultimately refused.

In frustration, Heldring tried to arouse interest for a more formal, structured approach to activities by *Réveil* circles. "What ought we to do?" asked his circular letter of 1845; "are we to continue our separate ways, or is united action possible?" This initiative resulted in biannual meetings in Amsterdam of a group of men who styled themselves the "Christian Friends." Usually chaired by Groen, these meetings were spent discussing projects, sponsoring activities, and raising funds. The cause of Christian education was also close to the hearts of the Friends. As well, one entire meeting was devoted to the question: Should Christians form a political party? We have no choice, was Groen's opinion; our constitutional system requires political alternatives. Those who hold to the same principles should band together and try to achieve their goals by proceeding according to well-devised plans to persuade voters and influence law-making. Christians are members of the Nation and as such have rights in the State, as well as consequent duties: namely, to uphold these rights and to fulfil these duties in communion with the brothers.

One result of these meetings was the appearance, from time to time, of anti-revolutionary voters' associations in urban ridings. Another was the regular publication, from 1847 to 1875, of *De Vereeniging: Christelijke Stemmen*, a quarterly edited by Heldring, with contributions in theology, history, literature, inner mission and philanthropy, as well as articles of political analysis and debate. After about a decade, however, the meetings in Amsterdam died out because the Christian Friends could not agree on a common stance against

I. Kuyper as Heir 21

the incursion of modernism in the National Church, some favouring a "juridical" approach (use the church courts to discipline, suspend or defrock offenders) while others favoured a "medical" approach (preach the full gospel, which alone is able, in time, to overcome its deniers). By this time, however, Abraham Kuyper had taken up the campaign for church reform in a robust combination of both strategies.

Johan Adam Wormser (1807–1862): abandoning establishmentarianism

This court bailiff from Amsterdam had his own approach to the challenge of modernity. In his book of 1853 on the meaning of infant baptism, *De Kinderdoop*, he argued that, factually, almost all Dutch people had received Christian baptism. This meant that the Dutch nation had been sealed into the covenant of grace and thus could lay claim to God's promises. The only thing wanting was that the nation in many respects was either ignorant or negligent of its part of the bargain: namely, to embrace that covenant and dedicate itself in all the ramifications of national life to God. Hence Wormser wrote: "Teach the nation to understand and appreciate the meaning of its baptism, and church and state are saved."[32]

Wormser agreed with Groen that the worst enemy in the battle for reasserting the Christian character of Dutch society

---

[32] J. A. Wormser, *De Kinderdoop, beschouwd met betrekking tot het bijzondere, kerkelijke en maatschappelijke leven* [Infant baptism considered in relation to personal, church, and social life] (Amsterdam, 1853), 8–9: "Leer dan de natie haar doop verstaan en waarderen, en kerk en staat zijn gered."

was the world-flight and politicophobia of orthodox Christians. As a result, the country was increasingly being brought "under the sway of the Revolution ideas and their destructive effects." This state of affairs must be turned around. After all, "the question is far from settled whether the nation, just as it formerly exchanged its pagan character for the Christian one, is now disposed to replace its Christian character with an atheistic one." And just because, he added defiantly, the revolution principles "have corrupted much, they do not have the right to corrupt *all* our institutions."[33]

Clearly Wormser was not yet ready, in the middle of the 19th century, to give up on the ideal of a Christian society. In more sober moments, however, Wormser would write to Groen that perhaps the situation had so altered that a radical reorientation was needed. He felt this to be true in particular for the struggle to keep the nation's schools Christian. He was by no means insensitive, he wrote, "to what is called the national church and our national schools and other institutions. The memory of what God in his grace has done in our land, and of the public institutions which arose as a result of that, always has much that is precious and appealing to me." But the problem was that amid much spiritual awakening and revival of individual people, the reformation and revival of time-honored institutions was proving much more difficult. In the growing conflict over the spiritual direction of Dutch society, the nominal Christian character of many institutions might well be removed by the Lord himself, and through the crisis the members of His Body could then grow to greater

---

[33] Ibid., 44.

I. Kuyper as Heir

solidity and independence.[34] By 1860, both Wormser and Groen, along with many others, divested themselves of the last remnants of thinking in terms of corporate Christianity and Constantinian establishment, to turn to free schools and a free church in a state that would grant favours to the adherents of neither modernism nor orthodoxy. This was to become the guiding idea of Kuyper's public theology.

And so gradually a pattern of *separatism* became visible that had really characterized the anti-revolutionary movement from its earliest beginnings. Thus, the so-called line of "antithesis" that ran right through the Dutch nation, making division between orthodox believers and all others, was not an invention of Abraham Kuyper. As early as 1841 Elout van Soeterwoude explained to an English anti-slavery activist why it was that Holland's evangelical Christians did not want to open their Abolition Society to "all men of good will" (as Wilberforce had been able to do in Britain) but instead felt compelled to limit membership to confessing Christians only. Time and again it has been our unhappy experience, Elout wrote, that such common undertakings end up banning the Christian basis of the work in favour of a kind of neutrality that lacks "the faith that can overcome the world."[35]

Elout was deploring the intolerance in his country that would soon go by the name of "anticlericalism." A few years after Elout's explanation, no professorial chair was made avail-

---

[34] Wormser to Groen, 1 April 1844; in G. Groen van Prinsterer, ed., *Brieven van J. A. Wormser*, 2 vols. (Amsterdam, 1874), I, 17–18.

[35] Elout to Rev. E. Miller, 7 Dec. 1841; in G. Groen van Prinsterer, *Briefwisseling*, V, 793–795.

able for Isaac da Costa in the City University of Amsterdam despite a long list of prominent names endorsing the nomination. The snub caused Groen to muse: if Christian principles cannot be brought to our public institutions, perhaps we will wake up to see the need for *our own institutions*.[36] He thus laid the seeds for the phenomenon of "pillarization," or, as I prefer to call it, "institutionalized worldview pluralism."[37]

Isaac Esser (1818–1885): educating the common people

Groen wrote tough, sinewy prose, in high-brow papers. Fortunately, popularizers of the anti-revolutionary worldview were not lacking. Of these, Isaac Esser, a soap-box evangelist in The Hague, deserves a brief mention. Esser had distinguished himself as an administrator in the Dutch East Indies, where he had combated corruption, prosecuted slave-trade, and actively promoted Christian missions among the natives.

---

[36] Groen to Da Costa, 16 Nov. 1844; in *Brieven van Da Costa*, I, 188–189 (emph. added).

[37] See my "Groen van Prinsterer's Interpretation of the French Revolution and the Rise of 'Pillars' in Dutch Society," in *Presenting the Past: History, Culture, Language, Literature*, series Crossways, vol. 3 (London: Centre for Low Countries Studies, University College, 1996), 83–98. Ever since I introduced the term, it has been the common designation for this peculiar phenomenon of cultural pluralism based on equal rights for competing fundamental commitments in a modern democracy. Note too that the pillars together shored up the national community. They competed with each other for popular support, but the pillars were no silos: they also communicated and at times cooperated with each other. See Part IV below for concrete instances of pillars.

I. Kuyper as Heir

Once repatriated, he joined actions against modernism in the national church. Unsuccessful in a bid for a seat in parliament in 1864, he threw himself into the renewed struggle for Christian day schools. His activities ranged from handing out tracts at fairgrounds during carnival season, to writing a weekly series of articles on a sound colonial policy, translating psalms into the Malay language, setting up a ragged school, and, later, serving on the Board of Governors of the Free University.[38]

The book *Unbelief and Revolution* had meant a great deal to Esser during disturbances in 1848 on Java. In his retirement he approached the author for permission to quote extensively from it in a primer that he was composing "for the people behind the voters." When Groen was shown a sample of the text, he advised Esser to abandon the method of using direct quotations and instead turn his "excellent talent for popularization" to good account by saying the same thing in his own words. The upshot was the appearance later that year of Esser's *Anti-revolutionaire Catechismus, ook voor het volk achter de kiezers*. The booklet has been called "a most peculiar publication in anti-revolutionary history."[39] It demonstrates "the conviction among Groen's supporters who followed Groen and prayed for him," that the anti-revolution in the country would be nothing if not a grass-roots movement involving thousands of (as yet non-voting) "ordinary" believers. Here are a few

---

[38] T. Smid, "Isaäc Esser," *Woord en Wereld* 3 (1966): 205–20, 302–311.

[39] J. van Wehring, *Het Maatschappijbeeld van Abraham Kuyper* (Assen: Van Gorcum, 1967), 53.

representative Questions and Answers from Esser's "anti-revolutionary catechism":

> *Question 1*: What is the infallible touchstone of all that is just and moral, both for nations and private persons? *Answer*: Holy Scripture! Unconditional submission to God's Word, to "it is written," is the warrant for both dutiful obedience and dutiful resistance, the guarantee of order and freedom.
>
> *Q. 2*: Are there any other tests of justice and morality? *Answer*: Undoubtedly! History and nature are also tests. Throughout the ages history and nature have taught [mankind] to start with God and to consult experience....
>
> *Q. 12*: Do only governments have divine right? *Answer*: By no means! All authorities are God's lieutenants, God's ministers—for your good, writes Paul. *We* are to obey them for the Lord's sake; *they* are to obey God. Superior power is a gift of God which is to be used in His service, to the benefit of others and to His honor. The Sovereign bears the image of God on earth, but this is nothing extraordinary or special which he has as a privilege above other people. A father bears the image of God to his child, a judge to the accused, a mistress to her maids. Anybody who is anything or has anything is an image-bearer of God, obligated and called, each according to his gift as a good steward, in the name and according to the example of our Lord, to walk in the good works which He has ordained for us....
>
> *Q. 24*: How does the anti-revolutionary see the French Revolution? *Answer*: As a work of unbelief and revolt, of apostasy from the living God and at the same time as a judgment of God.

Q. 25: How can you prove this? *Answer*: From the plain facts of the revolution. The tree is known by its fruit. . . .

Q. 47: Is the struggle of our day at bottom a religious struggle? *Answer*: No other. Underneath all the burning questions of our day lies the religious question. It all comes down to this: Who is sovereign, God or man?[40]

Unlike ruling elites who often underestimate the "common people," Esser was not afraid to tax their minds by feeding them food to chew on. Soon, Kuyper would deploy his talent in this medium and regale his followers—common folk like masons and blacksmiths, merchants and shopkeepers, farmers and farmhands—with witty political asterisms in his daily *De Standaard* and warm devotionals in his weekly *De Heraut*.

Klaas Kater (1850–1916): mobilizing the working classes

Listening to the contributions of leaders of the first and second rank, like Groen and Esser, we begin to realize that the anti-revolution was becoming a grass-roots movement. Many of the orthodox people belonged to the common folk who in a "census democracy" (as Holland then was) often lacked the property or income qualifications to have the right to vote. These "people behind the voters" still awaited their emancipation. Given this circumstance, of course, they were hardly empowered to participate in decision-making for the future—though not for lack of interest in politics and public affairs!

---

[40] I. Esser, *Antirevolutionaire Catechismus* (The Hague, 1874), 3, 7, 18, 48.

We hear of a cigar-maker's shop in Amsterdam, for example, where one of the workmen would read aloud from the writings of Groen while his fellow workers filled his quota during that time.[41]

The story of the emancipation of the working classes in the Netherlands includes many names, among which Klaas Kater figures large.[42] But it all began with another man—with Julien Wolbers (1819–1889), the owner of a painting and decorating firm in Harlem who retired early to devote himself to the promotion of the rising social movement which he wished to influence in a Christian direction.[43] In the summer of 1871, he started a weekly called *De Werkmansvriend*. Despite its patronizing name ("The Workingman's Friend") the weekly was well received by working-class people who could resonate with the opening editorial, which stated:

> The social question is the order of the day. The industrious workman has a right to claim that his wages be commensurate to his needs and those of his family, and that he ought

---

[41] Wormser to Groen, 27 August 1851; in *Brieven van Wormser*, I, 238.

[42] See R. Hagoort, ed., *Gedenkboek Patrimonium* (Utrecht, 1927), 104–135, 164–180; idem, *De Christelijk-sociale beweging* (Franeker: Wever, n.d. [1956]), 70–84. See also Paul E. Werkman, *"Laat uw doel hervorming zijn." Facetten van de geschiedenis van het Christelijk Nationaal Vakverbond in Nederland (1909–1959)* (Hilversum: Verloren, 2007).

[43] Werkman, *"Laat uw doel hervorming zijn!"* 24–26. See also "Wolbers, Julien" in *Biografisch Woordenboek van het Socialisme en de Arbeidersbeweging in Nederland.* URL: http://hdl.handle.net/10622/ 1BDB5785-1310-47D5-990B-A2800CA16183

not to suffer want or be forced to deny himself all physical relaxation and every opportunity to ennoble his mind.[44]

But, Wolbers continued, the improvement of the workingmen's lot depends on their own activity: what they need is "a healthy spirit of self-confidence, coupled with reliance on and invocation of higher blessing." The editor placed his hope in honest work, duty, piety, education, vocational training, mutual aid in case of illness, etc., "provided all this is pursued in a sound spirit of moderation and order, and not through violence." The paper would therefore combat that new manifestation of the Revolution in the world, the International, whose principles

> lead workmen to be discontented with their rank and lot, arouse their resentment against those more generously endowed with temporal goods, and excite them to resistance if not revolt. . . . Under the fine-sounding slogans of seeking to progress, of wanting to champion the rights of the workingman, to emancipate labour, to promote liberty, equality and fraternity, they are liberally sowing the seed which, according to our most sacred convictions, will only bear bitter—and for the workman himself most pernicious fruits. . . . The revolutionary movement is characterized by apostasy from God and the denial of His love and power. We,

---

[44] *De Werkmansvriend*, 28 Juli 1871. For this and the following quotations from *De Werkmansvriend*, see R. Hagoort, ed., *Patrimonium (Vaderlijk Erfdeel): Gedenkboek bij het gouden jubileum* (Utrecht, 1927).

by contrast, believe that only a turning back to God, acknowledging and obeying His Word, and sincerely believing in His grace in Jesus Christ, will promote the salvation, including the temporal well-being, of the workman, as of all men. Whatever proceeds from this spirit we shall advocate, and we consider baleful and shall combat whatever proceeds from a different spirit.

Against this background the paper announced its intention to be a clearing house for news about "such workingmen's associations which, averse to the criminal agitation of the International, aim to ameliorate the workman's lot in the gradual way of order and law, without violent upheavals." As he thus opposed the Revolution with the Gospel, Wolbers was pitting Groen against Marx.

Predictably, rival papers, sponsored by social democrats, warned against mixing "theology" with the social question. In reply, Wolbers reassured them that "no theological disputes, no sermons, no catechism" would appear in *De Werkmansvriend*.

> Yet we cannot imagine a society without religion. Where religion is lacking society will not thrive. We believe that the healing of our sick society and the well-being of the workingman cannot be attained except through a revival of religion and obedience to God's Word.

Accordingly, *De Werkmansvriend* intended to deal with the various social issues from a Christian standpoint, "and therefore not without regarding religion as one of the most important factors." In the present circumstances, they may not be silent observers who know in their hearts that "to forsake God and His service and no longer to honour His Word as the highest law" leads a people to the abyss.

One enthusiastic journalist who joined Wolbers as editor of *De Werkmansvriend* was Willem C. Beeremans (1852–1937). Beeremans was particulary interested in giving guidance to the rising labour movement. Writing in 1873 that what was needed was "a return to a Christian society," he asserted:

> there are no purely social questions. Every one of them, however many there be, must find their solution in Christianity, must be solved according to the demands of God's laws. . . . To be sure, workmen's associations are not religious gatherings . . . but is it just, is it fair, timidly to exclude or eschew all religion when discussing social issues?

Beeremans advocated looking to God's Word rather than "rallying under the red flag." While recognizing the legitimacy of labour unions and the need for social reform, he objected to a purely horizontal approach to these questions, noting in particular that the widespread negation of divine providence encouraged the working classes to attack the very foundations of society and to put all the blame for their present plight on employers and social institutions. We hear a great deal at union meetings about *brotherhood* and *love of neighbor*, he wrote, but no one remembers the first and great commandment: *to love God*.

But how "Christian" can trade-unions be? To those who objected that it would be out of the question, for example, to open union meetings with prayer, Beeremans retorted:

> Exactly! Herein lies the unhappy condition of our society. It has slid from the foundation of God's Word, on which it stood steady and firm, to place itself on another soil, in which it must sooner or later sink away... Unions will only be useful to the working class in particular and society in general if, there too, men would push their demands more into the background and ask first of all what God demands.

Another contributor to the weekly, Jacob Witmond (1832—1899), a trained evangelist turned journalist, soon joined Beeremans in his endeavor to arouse interest in a novel venture: organizing an avowedly Christian Workingmen's Association. Together they persuaded the Amsterdam labour activist, Klaas Kater, to join them.

This initiative would prove historic. Kater, a largely self-taught man, had written several candid contributions in *De Werkmansvriend* exposing poor wages and working conditions in a variety of firms which he mentioned by name. He had been president of a local bricklayer's union and had begun to play a leading role in the fledgling national federation of labour unions. However, he had felt compelled to resign from the latter when running into firm opposition to his idea of *samenwerking* (co-operation) with owners and management. Other reasons for his withdrawal were profanity, Sabbath desecration, and flirting with the Marxist International. For the time being, Kater was at a loss where else to work for labour reform.

I. Kuyper as Heir

Shortly thereafter, he felt vindicated in having left the national federation when, at the urging of Young Liberals on its board, it adopted a change in its constitution by which it came out strongly in support of the "promotion and extension of neutral public primary and secondary education." Kater now agreed, when approached by Beeremans and Witmond, that Christian workmen had no choice but to create an alternative by forming a parallel organization. To remain silent in the face of such "senseless demands," which liberals claimed were made on behalf of "the workingmen of Holland," was tantamount to "denying Christ [and] contributing to the ruin of our people as a Christian nation."

The three men called a meeting on 3 January 1876 where preparations were made for a distinctively Christian social organization embracing employers and employees and taking for its basis, direction, and goal "Him who is the centre of world history and outside of Whom there is no salvation." Out of this initiative was born the organization named "Patrimonium"—the name being indicative of the members' determination to stand on guard for the national Christian "heritage." In the very month that Groen lay dying—May 1876—a constitution was drafted, and an organization was launched that would represent the anti-Revolution in the world of labour.

Kuyper's *Standaard* at first did not pay much attention to this new development. On several occasions Kater complained to the editor-in-chief of being ignored.[45] Before long,

---

[45] Kater to Kuyper, Dec. 12, 1877; Aug. 8, Aug. 11, Nov. 10,

however, Patrimonium was the largest social organization in the Netherlands and could no longer be ignored. Although in later decades it would be eclipsed by separate organizations for workingmen and for employers, nevertheless a pattern was set: for the socio-economic sector, too, Holland's Christians (not the churches or the clergy but the "lay" people) ran their own distinct organizations in a bid, along with other-minded, parallel organizations (such as bread-and-butter unions and the social democratic movement) to influence the future conditions of the daily workplace. To this day, consociational democracy in the Netherlands is also reflected in the institutionalized worldview pluralism of its socio-economic sector.[46]

Our interest here lies with a number of distinct expressions and formulations found in Patrimonium's Constitution as well as in the commentary written by Kater, its first president. The founding fathers were very conscious of the fact that they were adding a new branch to the anti-revolutionary movement in the land. Thus, Article 1 stated that the organization accepted "God's Word and the traditions of our people as the trustworthy foundations of a Christian Society," and Article 2 listed among the means of promoting its aims: propagating its

---

1879; see letters in Kuyper-archief, Documentatiecentrum voor het Nederlands Protestantisme, Free University, Amsterdam.

[46] Cf. Michael P. Fogarty, *Christian Democracy in Western Europe, 1820–1953* (Notre Dame UP, 1957), chaps. xv-xviii; Arend Lijphart, *The Politics of Accommodation: Pluralism and Democracy in the Netherlands* (Berkeley: University of California Press, 1968), passim; Rob Nijhoff, "Christian Democracy in Neo-Calvinist Perspective. Central Motives, Historical Roots," *Sfera Politicii* 19/3 (2011): 18–22. URL: https://revistasferapoliticii.ro/sfera/157/art03-Nijhoff.php

principle, holding meetings, studying history, aiding widows and sick or injured workmen, sponsoring a popular book series, operating reading rooms and a library, and establishing trade schools and consumer and housing cooperatives. Curiously, an earlier pamphlet had specified for the library that it should be "a library in which, for example, the works of Groen van Prinsterer have a prominent place"—rather appropriate for an organization whose president had addressed its membership at the start of a meeting as "spiritual sons of the late lamented Groen van Prinsterer."[47] After Patrimonium received a royal charter on 19 March 1877, Kater was invited to introduce the new organization to the readers of *De Werkmansvriend*. In the issue of 6 April 1877, he emphasized that the guiding principle of Patrimonium in the social sector would be "*samenwerking*," co-operation with "*all* who acknowledged God and His Christ as the supreme ruler and whose aim in life was to glorify His Name," irrespective of the class to which they belonged. We demand to be recognized as members of society, he explained, as creatures who may not be suppressed or exploited. Class distinctions should be reduced, mutual aid encouraged, and injustices set right. By what means? Not by coercion, but by persuasion:

> We believe that the fate of the world is guided by an Almighty hand, wherefore we are unwilling to stretch forth the hands of violence to seize the property of others: nor do we wish, by resorting to compulsion when circumstances

---

[47] Quoted in Hagoort, ed., *De Christelijk-sociale beweging*, 52.

seem favourable to us, to appropriate to ourselves that which He has entrusted to others.

No doubt such phrases might have lulled some employers to sleep. But docility was not the intention. Boldly, Kater went on to address the structural violence embedded in an economy based on untrammeled free enterprise:

> But should the rich of this world wish to administer the goods entrusted to their stewardship exclusively to their own benefit, to use them solely for their own advantage, then we affirm that in this regard the doctrine of Proudhon is altogether true: "Property is theft." Hence we wish, in accordance with the Word of God, to testify against every form of violence that exalts itself against Him, whether it proceeds from workingmen or from whomsoever. Accordingly, we reject all strikes, as fruits of the revolution. But we also condemn every association of money or power entered into for the purpose of securing a monopoly.[48]

Kater had read his Groen well. The latter had been very critical of the new socio-economic developments inspired by liberalism. In a series of pamphlets of 1848 Groen had written:

> Our worst ailment is pauperism. Poverty, no work; ruptured relations between the higher and lower classes; no bond except wages and labour; proletarians and capitalists. Whither will this lead? That is uncertain. But there is no

---

[48] Quoted in Hagoort, ed., *Patrimonium (Vaderlijk erfdeel)*, 179.

I. Kuyper as Heir

doubt whence it came. It came from "Liberty and Equality" as understood by the Revolution. Just one detail. When that slogan was first raised, guilds and corporations too had to go. The desire was for free competition; no restraints on skills and industry; no hateful monopoly exercised by individuals or societies; then the development of private initiative and commerce would guarantee a better future. The future that was envisioned has arrived. Can it be called better? *I am of one voice here with the leading spokesmen of the present-day revolution.* It is this liberty, this unrestricted competition, this removal, as much as possible, of the natural relationship of employer and employee, which tears the social bonds, ends in the dominance of the rich and the rule of the banking houses, robs artisans of regular sustenance, splits society up into two hostile camps, gives rise to a countless host of paupers, prepares for the attack by the have-nots on the well-to-do and would in many people's eyes render such a deed excusable and almost lawful. It has brought Europe to a state so dreary and somber as to cause many to tremble and cry out: Is there no way to revive, in some altered form, the associations that were so recklessly crushed under the revolutionary ruins?[49]

As he echoed these sentiments—including his bow to Proudhon—Kater was not merely harking back to a radical outburst by his venerated statesman. His boldness was borne

---

[49] G. Groen van Prinsterer, *Vrijheid, Gelijkheid, Broederschap; toelichting op de spreuk der Revolutie* (The Hague, 1848), 83–84 (emph. added).

up by deep-seated convictions. His article of April 1877 in *De Werkmansvriend* concluded with these words:

> To this end we await the help of Him who has made the heavens and the earth, and we call out to all, be they rich or poor, of gentle or humble birth, employer and employee: Join us, so that our dear fatherland, our cherished royal house, and all inhabitants of these lands so richly blessed of God, may be preserved from the Spirit that is not of God, from the ruinous plans of the revolution.[50]

The new organization attracted many members. Here was a "brotherhood" that did not disregard their Christian loyalties but appealed to them! As well, Patrimonium's initiative in setting up housing cooperatives met a great need. Besides attending to social concerns, members also gave their support to the Anti-Revolutionary Party (ARP) when it was organized in 1879, hoping for a kinder dispensation someday. Often not voters themselves, they volunteered for election campaigns and helped round up voters on election day. Understandably, a little over a decade later, Patrimonium's leaders expressed grave disappointment at the slow progress in social reforms made by the first Anti-Revolutionary cabinet, the Mackay Ministry of 1888–1891. Our own parliamentarians, Kater stated forthrightly in his annual presidential address of Nov. 1890, don't feel our misery because they stem from the aristocracy. He added ominously: If the Anti-Revolutionary Party does not soon field some candidates from the working classes, our members are thinking of starting a

---

[50] Quoted in Hagoort, ed., *Patrimonium (Vaderlijk erfdeel)*, 180.

Christian Labour Party.[51] At this, Abraham Kuyper took alarm. At once he began to take steps towards organizing a Social Congress to address the social question in solidarity with all the brothers, of whatever class or station in life. There he would, in his opening address, call for "architectonic critique" of existing society.[52] There he would pray for the suffering masses with words that would be repeated on many lips afterwards: "They cannot wait, not a day, not an hour."[53]

Abraham Kuyper (1837–1920):
seizing the initiative

With that, we have come to the heir of all these personalities, voices, and publications—to the man who like no other succeeded in turning this rich tradition to political profit. The broad outline of Kuyper's career is familiar enough not to be repeated here, but it may not be superfluous to remind ourselves that he did not single-handedly, between the age of 35 and 49, create a daily newspaper, a political party, a separate university, and a new, orthodox Reformed denomination. In each case he was indeed a co-founder—a leader, organizer, inspirer, to be sure, but always surrounded by a score of peers

---

[51] *Jaarboekje van het Nederlandsch Werkliedenverbond Patrimonium* (Amsterdam, 1891), 81–85.

[52] Abraham Kuyper, *The Problem of Poverty*, ed. James W. Skillen (Grand Rapids, MI: Baker, 1991), 51. For a complete translation that includes the 109 endnotes, see today, Abraham Kuyper, *Collected Works in Public Theology: On Business and Economics* (Bellingham, WA: Lexham, 2021), 169–229.

[53] See my "How Abraham Kuyper Became a Christian Democrat," *Calvin Theological Journal* 33 (1998): 420–435.

who acted as Kuyper's collaborators and assistants, advisers, supporters, financiers, and critics. More to the point for us may be to listen to a statement of his deepest motivation. In 1897, looking back over his career thus far, Kuyper, then 60 years old, composed a little poem (adapting one, he explained, by Da Costa[54]), which he recited at a public reception honoring his 25-year editorship of *De Standaard*. In translation, the poem runs somewhat as follows:

> My life is ruled by but one passion,
> > one higher urge drives will and soul.
>
> My breath may stop before I ever
> > allow that sacred urge to fall.
>
> 'Tis to affirm God's holy statutes
> > in church and state, in home and school,
> > despite the world's strong remonstrations,
>
> to bless our people with His rule.
>
> 'Tis to engrave God's holy order,
> > heard in Creation and the Word,
> > upon the nation's public conscience,
>
> till God is once again its Lord.

---

[54] Cf. Isaac da Costa, *Kompleete Dichtwerken*, ed. Hasebroek, 8th impr. (Leiden: A. W. Sijthoff, n.d. [1898]), I, 201–202, stanza 10 in Da Costa's poem "Vrijheid": "Voor my! één doel slechts heeft mijn leven! / Één uitzicht vult geheel mijn ziel! / En moog my d' adem eer begeven, / dan dat dit uitzicht my ontviel! / 't Is: met der Dichtkunst geestverrukking / het Ongeloof en zijn verdrukking / omver te stoten van zijn' troon! / Hy, die de Goliaths doet treffen, / kan de aard van 't ongeloof ontheffen / door éénen dichterlijken toon!" Da Costa's sonnet expresses the hope that the ecstasy of his poetry may bring relief from unbelief and knock it off its throne.

I. Kuyper as Heir 41

After his two-stage conversion—first as a theology student, then as a young pastor—Abraham Kuyper determined that he wanted to master what he decided had been the strength of the core of the nation: historic Calvinism. He would revive the 16th century confession of Calvin and Beza, develop the theology of Voetius and the fathers of Dordt, and update the public philosophy of Hotman, Languet and Marnix. For obtaining works in the latter category he wrote to the best guide available: Dr. G. Groen van Prinsterer.

Groen responded by recommending instead authors whom he referred to as the "founding fathers" of *modern*, Christian-historical political thought, namely: Edmund Burke, François Guizot, and Friedrich Julius Stahl. For good measure, Groen also sent Kuyper complementary copies of his own works. Kuyper devoured them and began to "spread the word" in lectures to a student club in Utrecht, the place of his second charge as pastor, and to similar clubs in other university towns.

After Kuyper moved to Amsterdam and started his newspaper (made possible in part by Groen's munificence), there followed an amazing collaboration between the two publicists: in commentary on public affairs they passed the ball to each other, Kuyper in his daily *De Standaard*, Groen in his biweekly *Nederlandsche Gedachten*. On one occasion Kuyper wrote: "Thanks for your formulation on p. 203 of your latest instalment: it will be the text for my next talk to the students."[55] And thus was born Kuyper's earliest statement in

---

[55] Kuyper to Groen, 10 Nov. 1873; in *Briefwisseling*, VI, 468,

political philosophy: *Calvinism: Source and Safeguard of Our Constitutional Liberties.*[56] As a trained theologian, a church historian by predilection, and an ordained pastor by professsion, Kuyper gained national prominence especially as a talented journalist. Friend and foe read the scintillating editorials in *De Standaard*, a daily newspaper launched on 1 April 1872.

In late 1873, in a by-election for the Second Chamber in Gouda riding, sympathizers with Groenian politics and subscribers to *De Standaard* nominated—without the candidate's prior permission, as was quite customary—as their favoured candidate: "Dr. Abraham Kuyper, pastor in the Reformed Church of Amsterdam." The first round was inconclusive: 957 votes for the liberal candidate, 767 for Kuyper, and 599 for the candidate supported by Catholics and conservatives. Simply as a test of voter strength, it pleased Kuyper greatly, as it did Groen. The numbers even suggested that the run-off election might actually go Kuyper's way; would he then have to accept and leave the parsonage to enter parliament? Kuyper agonized over the possibility. Sure enough, the results on January 21 were: 1252 votes for the Liberal candidate, as against 1504 for the Anti-revolutionary. The simple test had turned into a personal dilemma. Kuyper's

---

473). The reference is to *Nederlandsche Gedachten* of 22 Oct. 1873, in which Groen had written: "In the Calvinist Reformation according to Holy Scripture, in the history of their and our martyrs' church, lies the source and safeguard of the blessings of which 1789 gives the treacherous promise and the wretched caricature."

[56] A. Kuyper, *Het Calvinisme, oorsprong en waarborg onzer constitutioneele vrijheden* (Amsterdam, 1873); Eng. trans. in James D. Bratt, ed., *Abraham Kuyper: A Centennial Reader* (Grand Rapids, Mich.: Eerdmans, 1998), 281–317.

soul-searching intensified; his correspondence with Groen shows that it took him a full three weeks before he accepted.[57] What held him back? He complained of lack of clarity and certainty about a concrete platform to stand on. "One thing would give me courage," he wrote the old man in The Hague; "if I had a set goal and could see a path plotted toward it." He continued: "Tomorrow I shall therefore set my thoughts on paper. Then I shall send these to you, to approve or put aside." Two days after came the "loose thoughts," as the writer himself called them. "You will appreciate my purpose," he wrote Groen. "Accepting a seat is to me like accepting a mandate, so I feel I must know what direction to follow and what to undertake. I cannot take *a leap in the dark*. So I beg indulgence for my sketch. If it is all wrong, tell me freely. But at least give me the assurance . . . that your prudence has gone over the thought of the young man." Thus spoke the pupil to his mentor. His "sketch" consisted of a memorandum of 1500 words and displayed its author's political instinct, foresight, boldness, and above all, principled pluralism. Here are some telling lines:

> We should distinguish between what the anti-revolutionaries pursue as a *party* and what they present as a *general* political program to the *nation*. Only like-minded men can work for the former; the latter can be promoted by men of all parties. The former could become the latter only if the whole nation were converted to anti-revolutionary principles.

---

[57] See my "Abraham Kuyper between Parsonage and Parliament," *The Kuyper Centre Review* 4 (2014): 171–186.

To anticipate the future, we ought to take our cue from the current situation, in which the conservatives are dying away, the liberals, drawing no recruits from the younger generation, are destined for one part to revert to conservatism, for the other to vanish into the radical wing, with the result that when the generation now being educated at our secondary schools and universities is ready to take its place in society it will no longer be possible to stop the triumph of revolutionary radicalism unless we at this early stage take position at the head of the movement and *seize the initiative* in further developing our constitutional forms in a strictly neutral [non-partisan] sense, in order to avert a development in a positively anti-Christian spirit. Failing to do this, we shall inevitably be forced by future developments into the corner of reaction, forfeit our influence on public opinion, and in the end find our shameful place between ultramontanists and conservatives.[58]

It is highly significant that Christian politics in Kuyper's mind was not an endeavor to establish a "Christian society" in some theocratic sense. Neither was it the work of a lay "pressure group" or "special interest group." Rather, as he put it, Christian politics "must offer a *modus vivendi* even to the opponent." The memo continued:

> Our basic principle may not be an attempt to impose Christianity by force, open or indirect, but rather should be

---

[58] From the "Memorandum presented to Dr. G. Groen van Prinsterer by A. Kuyper during the latter's deliberation re accepting a seat in the Second Chamber," 4 Feb. 1874; published in *Briefwisseling*, VI, 735–738 (ital. in the orig.).

I. Kuyper as Heir

the belief that if Christianity is to regain its free and unhampered place in society it is only in and through the conscience of the nation and of individuals that it shall rule and thereby liberate state and society.

For this reason, no demanding any privileges; no ignoring the new phase that political life has entered, in part due to the Revolution; no attempts at subverting our civil liberties, but an effort to make them sound and to graft them onto a better root.

Proceeding from these premises, the fact will have to be recognized that our present constitutional order ... has not kept pace with the evolution of political life at the grass-roots level; that is a sheet of ice underneath which the water has flowed away and lacks even the vitality to catch up to the political evolution the nation is undergoing.

From this it follows that our party (1) must take up position not behind but in front of today's liberalism; and (2) must characterize that liberalism as stationary and conservative, hence ought to choose as its objective a revision of the Constitution, not in a partial but in a general sense. Our party, too, must be *liberal*, but in contrast to revolutionary liberalism it must stand for a *Christian* liberalism, different in this sense that it seeks a liberalism not against or without Christ but returning thanks to Him, a liberalism not against or without a historic past but accepted as the fruit of that past, a liberalism not restricted to the confines of our Constitution but in place of that strait-jacket offering a garment in which the nation can breathe and grow freely.

To this end the Constitution is to be purged of whatever tends to cause the State, in spite of itself, to favour its own form of religion, which must necessarily be anti-Christian in character. Purged of whatever separates the State from the life of the nation. Purged of whatever restricts the free course of the Christian religion. Purged, finally, of whatever obstructs the free development of the organic life of the nation.

How would all this be applied concretely? Kuyper devoted a number of paragraphs to each of the major political issues. By way of illustration, this is how his paragraph on education begins:

> Education is to be under the direction, regulation, and inspection of the State. For higher education the State is to endow a state university with fixed assets, in order that it may develop itself as a corporation solely in accordance with the innermost law of scholarship. No appointment of professors by the State, only curators, by the Crown, from nominations. To the free universities which one may wish to establish in addition, the same benefits are to be assured in respect of titles and degrees, not as regards endowment. Only in this way can a Protestant university come into existence at Utrecht and a Roman Catholic one at 's-Hertogenbosch, as the vital centres of the two large elements of the nation....

No one knew if this vision was practicable or just a pipe-dream, but Kuyper accepted his seat in parliament and embarked on a round of feverish activity. His maiden speech was about the social question, in particular child labour. His proposal that the time was ripe for a full-fledged Labour Code

I. Kuyper as Heir 47

was mockingly dismissed.[59] He supported the Anti-School Law League, helped organize the People's Petition against the Liberal school bill of 1878, and in the following year achieved a national federation of anti-revolutionary riding associations or voters' clubs, resulting in the Anti-Revolutionary Party, with which local cells of the Anti-School Law League soon merged.

It is still a thrill to read the series of broad-ranging, brilliant articles of 1878–79 in which he explained the new party's political program.[60] They articulated an inspired vision for the public square by a student of Calvinism and a disciple of Groen (and, incidentally, an admirer of the British statesman Gladstone). The articles appeared in *De Standaard* between April 1878 and February 1879 and have been systematically analyzed by McKendree Langley in terms of Christian thought, long-term goals, and short-term electoral outcomes.[61]

Summary

In what ways did his inheritance define Kuyper as heir? Our conclusion is clear. He steeped himself in a tradition that

---

[59] See A. Kuyper, *Our Program: A Christian Political Manifesto* (Bellingham, WA, 2015), 344–350.

[60] Published together as *"Ons Program." (Met bijlagen).* (Amsterdam, 1879; 1307 pp. Abridged ed., 1880; 493 pp. Eng. trans. of the abridged edition: *Our Program* (see previous note).

[61] McKendree R. Langley, *Emancipation and Apologetics: The Formation of Abraham Kuyper's Anti-Revolutionary Party in the Netherlands, 1872–1880* (Ph.D. thesis; Westminster Theological Seminary, Philadelphia, 1995).

was nearly a century old, reaping where others had sown. He mobilized a people already armed, elaborated a worldview and a program of action already sketched, and accelerated a movement already in motion.

Of course, Kuyper was more than the sum of his inheritance, the upshot of historical antecedents, a vector of historical forces.[62] He was also unique. But only against the backdrop of his historical context are we able to assess just how unique Abraham Kuyper really was.

---

[62] Annie Verschoor Romein, a Marxist historian, comes close to depicting Kuyper as sociologically inevitable; see *Erflaters van onze beschaving*, 7th impr. (Amsterdam: Querido, 1956), 748–771. Even H. Colijn barely escapes a similar interpretation of Kuyper's historical significance in his *Levensbericht van Dr. A. Kuyper* (Kampen: Kok, 1923); it may have been against his better knowledge that Colijn signed off on the official obituary, which was ghost-written by Professor Gerretson; cf. C. Gerretson, *Verzamelde Werken*, ed. G. Puchinger, 7 vols. (Baarn: Bosch & Keuning, 1973–1987), VII, 141.

II. KUYPER'S HEIRS

A cultural form-giver like Abraham Kuyper, no surprise, had many successors who worked with his ideas and benefited from his achievements. Among our selection of heirs of Kuyper, each had a connection with the chief vehicle of Kuyper's legacy, the Anti-Revolutionary Party. Five had careers in politics and two in the academy. Of course, the latter could be multiplied by hundreds of thousands of others, since Kuyper's thought, his theology,[63] his teachings in public theology,[64] and his devotional writings[65] have—quite apart from the impact of the many excellent recent Kuyper studies in

---

[63] See today, Cory C. Brock and N. Gray Sutanto, *Neo-Calvinism: A Theological Introduction* (Bellingham, WA: Lexham Press, 2022). Still very useful is Cornelis van der Kooi and J. de Bruijn, *Kuyper Reconsidered: Aspects of His Life and Work* (Amsterdam: VU Uitgeverij, 1999).

[64] See today, Abraham Kuyper, *Collected Works in Public Theology*, 12 vols. (Bellingham, WA: Lexham Press, 2015–2022). See also Michael Wagenman, *The Power of the Church* (Middletown, DE: n. pub., 2018; idem, *Engaging the World with Abraham Kuyper* (Bellingham, WA: Lexham Press, 2019).

[65] See today, A. Kuyper, *Honey from the Rock: Daily Devotions from Young Kuyper*, ed. and trans. by James A. De Jong (Bellingham, WA: Lexham, 2018). De Jong notes (p. xiii) that these weekly devotionals number over 2,200.

English [66] —permanently and profoundly influenced and shaped the thinking of scholars around the world, not to mention the faith, worldview, and outlook on life of a countless number of non-academics.[67]

L. W. Chr. Keuchenius (1822–1893): formulating an ethical colonial policy

A remarkable instance of the practical effect of anti-revolutionary politics is found in one of Kuyper's older contemporaries, Keuchenius (rhymes with *cutaneous*).

Born of Dutch parents in Batavia [Djakarta], Indonesia, Levinus Wilhelmus Christiaan Keuchenius was educated in the mother country where he earned his doctorate in law at Leyden before the age of 20. Following a brilliant career in Java as barrister and judge, he returned to Europe for health reasons and in 1866 became a member of parliament for the Anti-Revolutionary Party. Almost immediately his reputation as a parliamentarian was established when he saw his motion pass the Second Chamber censuring an ill-conceived government appointment for the colonies. Rather than resign, the Government called an election to campaign against this "encroachment upon the royal prerogative." The polls, however, returned the opposition members, who stuck to their

---

[66] Johan Snel, *The Seven Lives of Abraham Kuyper: Portrait of an Enigmatic Statesman* (Lexham Press; forthcoming).

[67] A complete bibliography of Kuyper's writings is found in Tj. Kuipers, *Abraham Kuyper: An Annotated Bibliography, 1857–2010* (Leiden: Brill, 2011), 756 pp.

guns. After two years of wrangling, the principle of responsible government was once for all established.[68]

Keuchenius' uncompromising stance contributed to a victory of fundamental significance. Conservative leaders, hiding as it were behind the Throne, had tried to force through their program in defiance of Parliament. And they had failed! How different European history would have turned out if, in a parallel case, the same dogged determination had been shown in these very years by the opposition in neighbouring Prussia! There, Bismarck ignored the majority in the *Landtag* and proceeded to modernize the country's military forces, financing expensive reforms by dipping without legislative approval into the national treasury. After the smashing Prussian military victory over Austria in 1866, the "Iron Chancellor" was forgiven: by legal enactment he was retroactively indemnified. The diplomacy of power politics now enabled Bismarck to provoke a war with France and establish a united German Empire under authoritarian rule imbued with a militant nationalism. Ask the French and the Brits where that led to.

Throughout the 1880s Keuchenius, finding moral support in Kuyper's earlier stance on colonial policy,[69] carried on a personal crusade against a particularly offensive instance of

---

[68] G. J. Schutte, "Keuchenius als minister van Koloniën," in Th. B. F. M. Brinkel, J. de Bruijn and A. Postma, eds., *Het Kabinet Mackay; opstellen over de eerste christelijke coalitie (1888-1891)* (Baarn: Arbor, 1990), 192–223, at 194.

[69] Kuyper's speeches in parliament regarding colonial policy have been published in A. Kuyper, *Eenige Kameradviezen uit de jaren 1874 en 1875* (Amsterdam: Wormser, 1890), chapters 1 to 10.

exploitation by Europeans in the Far East. A tin mining company, Biliton, had for more than thirty years enjoyed so favourable a contract with The Hague that it made millions while neither the Colonial Government nor the native people had enjoyed any profits to write home about. Eventually, after years of debate and an official enquiry, the Dutch parliament was able to reverse the situation.

Keuchenius likewise campaigned in favour of phasing out the Compulsory Cultivation System which had been imposed on Java earlier in the century by a greedy Mother Country. At the same time, however, he raised his voice to protest a growing movement to open the Colonies to private enterprise; he did not want to be party to replacing mercantilist opportunism with capitalist exploitation.

From 1888–1890 Keuchenius served as Minister of Colonial Affairs. His bills and other measures aimed to abolish opium licenses, raise wages on coffee plantations, lower land rents, restrict seignorial duties, reduce taxes, and (hardest of all) retreat from the war of aggression against the Sultan of Achin in Northern Sumatra. In short, he worked (a) to give up the annual profit on the balance sheet of the Colonial Office, and (b) to reverse the policy of imperialist expansion. In so doing, he inaugurated what his party would develop into an "ethical" policy for the colonies. This policy regarded Indonesia as a ward deserving of modern educational and medical facilities and a careful development of its natural resources to enhance its economic prosperity, to be followed by home rule and eventually full independence. Above all, the ethical policy was aimed at reversing the policy of favouring Islam for administrative and commercial reasons: the East Indian islands were to be opened to Christian missions, lest the native peoples be denied exposure to the message of the Christian gospel—a cause that was always very close to Keuchenius' heart. After his death, Kuyper wrote his biography, in which he remarked on the obvious piety and integrity that had stamped his political career.[70]

When he formed his cabinet in 1901, Kuyper made sure that the Speech from the Throne included a pledge that the Netherlands would work to fulfill "a moral duty with respect to the people of the colonies."

Alexander Idenburg (1861 – 1935): christianizing the public ethos

Under future Christian Ministries the anti-revolutionaries would have the opportunity of realizing more of Keuchenius' aims. The career of the statesman Alexander Willem Frederik Idenburg began when he served as a young officer with the corps of engineers in the Dutch East Indies, followed by ten years as department head with the Office of Defence in Batavia. Kuyper prevailed upon him to stand for election in 1901 and when he won his seat it was an informed "Indian specialist" that entered the Dutch Parliament.

In his maiden speech, Idenburg argued that the wealth of the Indies should benefit its own population and that the Netherlands owed it a moral and spiritual education in order to guide it to eventual political autonomy. Thus far, he lamented, we have given it the fruits of our civilization without its roots. To christianize India should not be seen as the

---

[70] A. Kuyper, *Mr. Levinus Wilhelmus Christiaan Keuchenius* (Harlem: Tjeenk Willink, 1895).

private hobby of some but as a matter of the highest political importance for all. This mission, however, should not be undertaken by the government but must be left to the churches. The task of the government was to remove by law all existing barriers and impediments to evangelization.[71]

In the mother country, Idenburg was Minister of Colonial Affairs during three separate terms (1902–05, 1908–09, and 1916–19). In between, he served abroad as Governor of Suriname (1905–08) and as Governor-General of the East Indies (1909–16). He finished a distinguished career in politics as a member of the Council of State, from 1924 till his death in 1935. He had the reputation, with friends and opponents alike, both in Europe and overseas, of being a gentle man of irenic disposition, uncommonly meek and mild for a former soldier, but standing firm on his principles and solidly grounded in personal faith and reliance on God.

Idenburg held to an enlightened version of the White Man's Burden. He disavowed modern imperialism if it meant conquest after conquest for profit and glory. But given our historic presence in the Far East, he explained in his maiden speech as cabinet minister, I can have peace with the term "imperialism" if it means benign rule in defence of legitimate interests and longstanding rights—if it means that we cannot avoid conflict, for example, with those who wish to perpetuate unjust and often inhuman conditions; who raid our frontiers; whose mismanagement provokes our intervention and whose misrule necessitates annexation; whose breach of contract

---

[71] For this and the following paragraphs, see *Ter Nagedachtenis aan Zijne Excellentie A. W. F. Idenburg* (Kampen: Kok, 1935); supplement to *Antirevolutionaire Staatkunde*, vol. 11 (April 1935).

compels us to use force, also with a view to protecting rightful foreign interests within our overseas possessions.[72]

During the defence of his first India budget, 20 Nov. 1902, Idenburg maintained that the Netherlands must do all it can to help elevate a population suffering from illiteracy, poverty, and disease. It should therefore stimulate in a powerful way the economic development of islands so rich in resources, for the benefit of its own peoples. At the same time, a policy of christianization must be pursued. By "christianization," he reassured his audience, he did not mean: giving people a personal saving faith, for no one can do that—no government and no missionary. But the aim of the government's policy was to turn the national spirit around, so that Christian values, like a leaven, would come to be accepted as part of the public ethos and the foundation of public life. To that end, Christian mission deserved the full protection of government.

In the same session of parliament Idenburg defended a bill to decentralize the colonial administration. It was his hope that the transfer of powers to lower organs would ensure that decisions affecting local needs and interests benefitted from local input. In this way he wanted to contribute to the coming of eventual Home Rule. At his installation as Governor-General in Batavia, 18 December 1909, he stated his belief that government, as the minister of God, is called to uphold the law and to administer justice. In this way alone could Dutch rule be a blessing to the people. He coveted the advice and

---

[72] Unlike Keuchenius, Idenburg defended the Dutch war on Achin because by this time the Sultanate of Achin harbored pirates who molested international shipping in the Strait of Malacca.

counsel, not only from the Dutch civil service, but also from the Indonesian population itself. I accept this high office, he concluded, "with a prayer for the blessing of Him who is the Fountain of all wisdom and strength." Words like these had never been heard on Java before.

At his departure from Batavia, 21 March 1916, Idenburg reminded his successor of the awakening of Asia. He himself had been open to native initiatives (provided they were orderly and peaceful) for greater participation in government, for he firmly believed that "authority and freedom must develop in harmony." The farewell speech shows Idenburg's hope of a future Netherlandic Commonwealth of Independent Nations, associated by a common allegiance to the House of Orange.

Back in the Netherlands, where he held a seat in the First Chamber for some years, he developed his constitutional views further. Someday our historic mandate will end, he held forth. External legal ties must make way for an organically grown cultural bond. Far too much, he lamented, has Dutch rule imposed a process of secularization on Indonesian society, replacing a sacral way of life with a mundane materialism. Indigenous movements can help alter this dangerous trend. But the inner strength of Islam and the ancient Hindu values must be deemed inadequate. Only Christianity can regenerate a people and develop its culture with lasting results. On that basis East and West can meet and together benefit the people. Such a fusion cannot be achieved by government but only by Christian missions and personal Christian testimony.

Did Idenburg himself act in harmony with these lofty goals? His government measures are a matter of historical record. In Suriname he stimulated the development of banana, sisal and rubber plantations while also restricting the use of opium and alcohol and promoting Sunday observance. In Indonesia he combated economic exploitation of the natives by Dutch planters and businessmen and abolished seigneurial duties and compulsory cultivation of coffee. On Java he established a school of commerce, a medical school, and a normal school or teacher's college. He put an end to the favoured treatment of secular government schools over private Christian schools. He granted permits to local—later also to wider—Islamic political organizations. He abolished casino permits and opium licences and promoted Sunday observance for the civil service. He restricted the practice of concubinage among Dutch military personnel. He regulated customary (heathen) law to accommodate native Christians, and he removed the last barriers to Christian mission on East Java, Sumba and Flores. With measures such as these Idenburg sought to promote the "christianization" of the Dutch "overseas possessions." No doubt he realized that it was no more than a beginning of implementing Kuyper's "ethical policy," but a turnabout had been made.

Syb Talma (1864–1916): democracy under the rule of Christ

As he grew up in a country that was gradually becoming more industrialized, the young theology student Aritius Sybrandus Talma deplored the liberal economics of the Manchester School with its unrestricted competition and its raw deal for the working classes. He devoured the books by the Christian

Socialists in Britain, Charles Kingsley and F. D. Maurice, who advocated consumer and producer cooperatives.[73]

Ordained in 1888 as a pastor in the National Reformed Church, his interest in the social question only increased. His first, rural parish contained many young farmers, to whom he talked not only about spiritual things but also about daily material concerns; together they studied historic revolts and their implications, including the French Revolution. When registering for the Christian Social Congress in 1891, he noticed that all participants were expected to express agreement with the Program of the sponsor of the congress, the Anti-Revolutionary Party. As he studied this document and Dr. Kuyper's extensive commentary *Ons Program*, he came to a startling realization: Kuyper offered in a Dutch "translation" what he had found in the Christian Socialists of Britain. He had been an anti-revolutionary all along!

Upon returning from the Social Congress, Talma put denominational sensitivities aside and joined what in his eyes was "the party of Dr. Kuyper" (who earlier had led the *Doleantie* breakaway from the national church). Talma also bypassed a Christian workmen's league recently endorsed by his denomination's Synod and instead took out membership in the "laymen's organization" *Patrimonium*, becoming editor-in-chief of its weekly paper not long afterwards. These preferences indicate that Talma kept Church and Christian action apart.[74]

---

[73] See Lammert de Hoop and Arno Bornebroek, *De rode dominee: A. S. Talma* (Amsterdam: Boom, 2010).

[74] See J. M. Vellinga, *Talma's sociale arbeid* (Hoorn: Edecea, 1941), 8–9.

II. Kuyper's Heirs

The elections of 1894 found Talma campaigning on behalf of widening the franchise. In a speech entitled "Mammon Suffrage or Manhood Suffrage," given in Dordt riding in support of candidate Kuyper, he uttered the oft quoted words: "Democracy will only be safe if it lets itself be ruled by Christ. It is up to us to prove that its ideals are secure with Him."[75] As he explained in a letter the following month:

> I agree as little with divine-right government as with laissez-faire economics. We must discover the *constitutio divina* for state and society. I am sceptical about detailed Christian programs and demands, but I also oppose individualism. We still lack a social creed. Since the 1850s, the Christian Socialists in Britain have achieved more than in Germany or France, but only after their message fell into the ground like a grain of wheat and died. The practical effect of our principles is a historical process, which we do not control....
>
> ... It is true, one must rebuke sin in both rich and poor.... But who shares the greatest blame today for our social woes? I feel pity for the masses whose spiritual and intellectual development is harmed by the wretchedness of their material conditions, and this pity makes us bitter at times when we pastors daily come into contact with disgusting phariseeism among the well-to-do.[76]

---

[75] For remarkably similar expressions, see Eustace Percy of Newcastle, *The Heresy of Democracy* (London, Eyre & Spottiswoode, 1954.)

[76] Talma to Lohman, 24 May 1894; quoted in H. van Malsen,

One Sunday afternoon—it was in Flushing, his second congregation—Talma got drawn into a public debate with the leader of the anarchist-socialists, Domela Nieuwenhuis. At the end of the hour he said: "If you want to hear more about the Christian view of man, come to church this evening." That evening several anarchists listened to a freshly made sermon by Rev. Talma on Isaiah 13:12: "I will make a man more precious than fine gold; even a man than the golden wedge of Ophir."

In the city of Arnhem, his third parish, Talma made himself available for the working classes, speaking in meetings of trade-unions and teaching evening courses. He also supported the local "midnight mission," helping the Committee against Prostitution by picketing houses of ill repute. In his frequent addresses to meetings of temperance unions he would emphasize that "the fight against alcoholism is a fight for the working classes." He was thoroughly familiar with every aspect of that question by the time he presided over the 13th International Congress against Alcoholism that met in The Hague in 1911. Talma was no single-issue activist.

In 1901, in the electoral sweep by the Christian parties, Talma unseated the social-democratic leader Troelstra in a hotly contested race in a Frisian riding. Once involved in the political process, Talma proved a man of practical measures.[77]

Alexander Frederik de Savornin Lohman (Haarlem: Bohn, 1931), 115–20.

[77] Cf. J. A. de Wilde and C. Smeenk, *Het volk ten baat; de geschiedenis der Anti-revolutionaire Partij* (Groningen: Jan Haan, 1949), 161, 193, 203, 209, 214, 243–49, 275–302. E. H. Kossmann, *The Low Countries*, 1780–1940 (Oxford: Clarendon Press, 1978), 499—501.

II. Kuyper's Heirs 61

His capacity for detail put him in the chair of the house committee for studying Kuyper's Temperance Bill. When the wildcat railway strikes broke out in late January 1903 and the Kuyper Ministry announced its countermeasures to safeguard the public interest,[78] Talma toured the country speaking out against a call for a general strike as a political weapon. That April, he was made chairman of the Parliamentary Inquiry into the conditions of streetcar personnel. Later that year followed his appointment to a study committee of the ARP to prepare recommendations for franchise reform.

Although the Christian parties lost their majority in 1905, Talma managed to retain his seat. Under a Liberal cabinet he chaired the house Defence Committee. This experience enabled him to contribute significantly to the great naval debates of 1907.

Under Prime Minister Theo Heemskerk (1908–1913) came the period of Talma's greatest activity. Serving as Minister of Agriculture, Commerce and Industry, he extended government aid to small manufacturers, set up industrial patent bureaus, and promoted a significant increase in vocational schools and experimental stations. As a lawmaker he was tireless. He personally drafted[79] and then defended a record number of social legislation bills, albeit with mixed success. He saw

---

[78] Cf. McKendree R. Langley, *The Practice of Political Spirituality: Episodes from the Public Career of Abraham Kuyper, 1879–1918* (Jordan Station, Ont.: Paideia, 1984), 91–101.

[79] This earned him a public rebuke from Kuyper, who had wanted Talma to save precious time by simply reviving Kuyper's raft of social legislation bills which had died on the Order Paper in 1905.

the passage of a fiercely debated Compulsory Social Insurance Act, for which employees would pay premiums in the form of a payroll deduction, entitling them to income during old age and in case of ill health or disability and thus avoiding the semblance of a free government handout. Also approved was his Stonemasons Act, which reduced working hours and prescribed rest periods and medical examinations. In other measures he was ahead of his time. His proposal for self-regulating Industrial Councils was voted down, and he was also forced to withdraw his Bakers Act when his own party, Kuyper first of all, argued that prohibiting night hours for bakery owners was an "attack on private enterprise" and a breach of "sphere sovereignty." He did, however, safely guide through parliament a reform of the Labour Act that further reduced the workday for women and youths to 10 hours and prohibited factory work for those below the age of 13. Unfortunately, the debate of his Longshoremen Bill, curtailing working hours and Sunday labour, was cut off by the dissolution of parliament that year.

Exhausted, Talma did not run for re-election but "retired" to a village parsonage. When the Great War broke out he accepted an appointment as chaplain-at-large to serve the boys in the mobilized army. Two year later he was dead, age 52. His life was spent defending the common man against, as he once put it, "a burden that would hinder him in living to the glory of God in accordance with human rights and personal aptitude." Our workingmen, he pleaded, must have time for more than work, work, work; they are husbands and fathers and church members and so much more. Talma opposed state socialism because it killed incentive, and he defended free enterprise but within limits, to prevent exploitation and abuse: active state intervention was the need of the hour, while government regulation at the same time should aim at restoring and promoting citizens' self-help. Outside parliament Talma toiled for the moral elevation of the working classes. He believed that this could not be achieved without a well-organized, powerful labour movement, but to be effective, it was best if Christian workingmen organized separately in distinctly Christian associations where they could work freely at the demanding task of developing a "social creed" and Christian social practices.[80]

Alexander Frederik de Savornin Lohman (1837–1924): true educational pluralism

Lohman, long Kuyper's associate in church reform and party politics, differed with the latter on many issues, also on the desired resolution of the schools struggle. While Kuyper fought for a negotiated settlement in a process of hard bargaining, Lohman took a higher moral ground. It is the Liberals who brought us school discrimination, he argued; therefore it is the Liberals who must be allowed to work out a mutually acceptable solution.

The solution came at last, in 1917, the year of the revision of the Constitution. The revision was in the nature of a "pacification" between Christian democrats and liberal democrats and paved the way for at least two momentous changes for which enough support was found on both sides: (1) universal

---

[80] For further details, see Vellinga, *Talma's sociale arbeid*, 7–20, 195–203.

suffrage: all males over 20 were given the vote; (2) full equality of all school systems: private parochial and parental schools as well as government schools were to receive public funding on a parity basis, subject to regular inspections and licensed teachers.

This last reform came close to recognizing the principle that private schooling was to be considered the normal rule and government schooling merely supplementary. Full parity was enshrined in the Education Act of 1920, which took effect in 1922. Before the decade was out, the public system was outstripped by the private schools, and today 75 per cent of Dutch children are educated in private schools. Such a statistic is indicative of the fact that for Dutch parents, the *choice* of school, whether it be for a secular, theosophist, Montessori, Catholic or Protestant school, does not depend on their financial means.

Jan Schouten (1883−1963): discerning the revolution in modern dress

We now come to what must be one of the most dramatic episodes in our historical survey. In the 1930s, Christians in the Netherlands, as elsewhere, were confronted by the "Twentieth-Century Revolution." As more and more European states embraced either socialism on the left or totalitarian regimes on the right, it almost seemed to the Dutch that the only viable choice for the future was . . . communism or fascism! Fortunately, one of their leading politicians publicly pronounced a plague on both their houses.

Jan Schouten had started out as a farmhand but through night classes worked himself up to become the leader of the Anti-Revolutionary caucus in parliament. In a pre-election

II. Kuyper's Heirs

kick-off speech[81] he pleaded with voters to reject the choice between communism or fascism as a false dilemma. Intimately acquainted with the plight of the common man and not afraid to call for tough measures to combat hard times, Schouten realized that to many people some form of authoritarian rule looked attractive as a solution to the chronic economic depression of the thirties. But he warned: Do not be deceived: modern dictatorships are long on promises but short on delivery! He buttressed his arguments with several lengthy quotations from Groen's *Unbelief and Revolution*, in a withering attack on "benevolent" dictatorship in all its forms. States like that, he explained,

> are products of the Revolution, fruits of the modern spirit that arose from a haughty indifference to God and a callous disregard for Divine law. Stalin and Hitler are like Robespierre and Napoleon, only worse so. Since all dictators must begin by denying the supreme rule of the Deity, they proceed to deify the State, maintain it by brute force, and end by destroying all liberty: they first abolish your political liberties; then they gradually abolish all your civil rights; and in the end they destroy your intellectual and moral freedom.

What practical effect could Schouten's address hope to have? It was not a political sermon delivered from a pulpit in some local parish. Nor was it an indignant letter to the editor

---

[81] Address to the national convention of AR delegates, held in Utrecht, 9 April 1937; text in *Geen vergeefs woord* (The Hague: Kuyperstichting, 1951), 322–333.

of some local newspaper. It was a speech by the leader of Kuyper's party, meeting in a national rally attended by the press. Schouten's speech enjoyed wide coverage throughout the country. In the ensuing elections, the National Socialists dropped from 8% to 4% of the popular vote, while the Anti-Revolutionary Party rose from 13 to 16 seats in the Second Chamber. Numbers like these, lost and gained in an existing multi-party system, though marking no landslides, pointed to significant shifts in voter support.

Kuyperians were forewarned as World War II drew closer. Their Synod declared membership in the political parties of the NSB (fascists) and the CDU (pacifist-socialist) to be incompatible with membership in the church of Jesus Christ.

Victor Henri Rutgers (1877–1945): confronting the modern dictator

The Second World War hit Holland in 1940. On May 10, the German Wehrmacht overran the country with lighting speed, and by the end of the month a German civil government was installed in The Hague. Although a solemn promise was made to respect existing Dutch laws and institutions, a slow but resolute program of *Gleichschaltung* ("coordination"; read: Nazification) was set in motion. The press, the arts, broadcast, youth movements—all had to toe the line ideologically and be assimilated in the "New Order."

In the second year of the German occupation, political parties were banned, but before the ban took effect the Anti-Revolutionary Party had tripled its paying membership, thanks in part, no doubt, to the strong leadership it had given from the start in immunizing the people against Nazi indoctrination. The widespread resistance movement that arose clandestinely

II. Kuyper's Heirs

counted a disproportionate number of Kuyperians among its members.[82]

The Occupiers made the mistake of attacking the school system. They ruled that Christian schools too needed to have all appointments to the teaching staff approved by the Education Ministry. "But that would be unconstitutional!" protested Professor Rutgers of the Law Faculty of the Free University.[83] Since the German occupier wanted above all to be viewed as decent and proper, this protest seemed to make some impression. Yet in the end, of course, the learned jurist's objection did not prevail against the Berlin-dictated policy of cleansing the schools of possible influences hostile to the regime. The boards were notified that all future appointments could be subject to veto by the Ministry in The Hague.

At this critical juncture non-government education showed its strength. Rutgers and others dispensed advice, preachers and priests mounted their pulpits, Protestants and Roman Catholics consulted together to offer a united front. In the end, mounting resistance—the ruling was ignored, or children were kept at home—eventually made the Occupier give up.[84]

---

[82] L. de Jong, *Het Koninkrijk der Nederlanden in de Tweede Wereldoorlog*, 14 vols. (The Hague: Staatsuitgeverij, 1969–1991), VII, 1014 (pop. ed.).

[83] De Jong, *Het Koninkrijk der Nederlanden in de Tweede Wereldoorlog*, V, 343 (pop. ed.).

[84] Cf. Th. Deleman, ed., *Opdat wij niet vergeten; bijdrage van de Gereformeerde Kerken in het verzet tegen het nationaal-socialisme en*

Rutgers was involved on many other fronts of defiance and resistance. Already in 1935 he had been a critical participant in the Berlin Conference on Criminal Law.[85] During the late thirties he was a driving force behind the Protestant Committee for Aid to Refugees on Account of Race or Religion,[86] and during the wartime occupation he continued his opposition to the Occupier's undermining of the rule of law. At one point, in the chief journal of jurisprudence, he openly urged judges to resign if forced to apply German enactments contrary to Dutch statute law or universal standards of equity. This bold advice he based on the argument from international law that military conquerors do not enter into the full rights of the

---

de Duitse tyrannie (Kampen: Kok, 1949), 87–92. A personal account of the wartime schools struggle is found in J. Overduin, *Hel en hemel van Dachau* (Kampen: Kok, 1947); Eng. trans., *Faith and Victory in Dachau* (Jordan Station, ON: Paideia, 1977). A scholarly treatment of the same subject was written by J. C. H. de Pater, *Het Schoolverzet, 1940–1945* (The Hague: Nijhoff, 1969).

[85] See his report in *Tijdschrift voor Strafrecht* 46.1 (1936): 59ff. Nazi Germany, he pointed out, is abandoning the golden rule, *nullum poene sine lege:* no punishment without a law. The conferees were taken on several excursions to penal institutions and addressed by German officials and top Nazi Party leaders. Rutgers was accompanied on this trip by his junior colleague, Prof. Herman Dooyeweerd, whose impressions, including an appraisal of fascist justice, are found in the journal of the Protestant Rehabilitation Society, *Orgaan* 4 (1936): 41–44, 50–53, 57–60.

[86] Rutgers was instrumental in the founding of Camp Westerbork as a temporary shelter for incoming refugees entering the Netherlands. In 1942, in a horrid irony of history, the German authorities converted Westerbork into a transit camp for Dutch Jews in preparation for "resettlement in the East."

II. Kuyper's Heirs

governments of a defeated state while a state of war exists. Rutgers reminded his fellow Dutch jurists that a legitimate government, which may command its citizens in all things lawful, must be distinguished from a government of conquest which is severely limited in the measures it may impose.[87] For good measure he added: "It is a distinction which we learned from Groen van Prinsterer"—and Rutgers proceeded to quote the entire "crowned-robber passage" from *Unbelief and Revolution* in which Groen had stated unequivocally: "I will not subscribe to any interpretation [of Romans 13] that would oblige us to be obedient to the villain who holds a dagger under our nose, or to hail today as a power ordained of God the crowned robber who yesterday banished our legitimate prince."[88]

Rutgers was imprisoned for several months when caught working for the (by then underground) Anti-Revolutionary Party. Tragically, he was again arrested during his flight to England crossing the North Sea in a small boat. His life ended in a German prison.

Herman Dooyeweerd (1894–1977): a new critique of theoretical thought

Dooyeweerd was born in Amsterdam in a "Kuyperian home" where Kuyper's daily *De Standaard* and his weekly *De Heraut* were read from cover to cover. After earning his D.Jur. degree

---

[87] Rutgers appealed to the 1907 Genevan Convention "Respecting the Laws and Customs of War on Land."

[88] V. H. Rutgers, "Toetsingsrecht" [Judicial Review], *Nederlandsch Juristenblad*, 29 Nov. 1941, 749–760, at 751, quoting *Ongeloof en Revolutie* (2nd ed., Amsterdam, 1868), 46f.

at the age of 23, he served for some years as a civil servant, until he accepted the post of assistant director of the Abraham Kuyper Institute, the administrative headquarters, think-tank, and clearing house of the Anti-Revolutionary Party, located in The Hague in what used to be Kuyper's own house and last home. As he settled into his job, Dooyeweerd was to experience a turning point in his life. This is how he remembered it during a radio interview[89] in his old age:

> When I came to the Kuyper Institute I felt it was incumbent upon me to start reading and studying what Kuyper had written. That may seem obvious, but I didn't feel much like it because in my youth ... all you ever heard was Kuyper and more Kuyper, and in my student days I tended to be rather critical, and so on. But I started to read him with serious intent. And one afternoon, as if by accident (which we know is never an "accident")—it was already past four o'clock and I was working in Kuyper's old study, sitting at his enormous old desk—I happened to notice a stack of little books. I picked the first one that came to hand and saw that it contained meditations on Pentecost.[90] I would never have picked up a booklet like that earlier in my life, but I thought to myself: I ought to take a look at what he made of such meditations. I started to read, and four hours later I was still there! I was so moved by what Kuyper had to say in these

---

[89] Interview with Ph. Engelen, broadcast on IKON radio, May 16, 1973. Official transcript, with a translation by Jack Van Meggelen, in the Dooyeweerd Centre, Redeemer University.

[90] A. Kuyper, *Dagen van goede boodschap*, 4 vols. (Amsterdam: Wormser, 1887–88). Vol III: *Op den Pinksterdag*.

II. Kuyper's Heirs

mediations that I realized: this is a completely different Kuyper from the one we know from his theological works.

You see, in theology he is scholastic, but not at all in these meditations. Here he has vibrant biblical thoughts. And what particularly grabbed me at that moment was that Kuyper had again discovered something that had been completely lost in scholasticism. What had been lost was the biblical view of man—that the centre of man's life lies in his heart, in the core of his existence. But when people spoke about what the Bible means by the image of the heart, they usually took it to be the seat of the emotions, for example in expressions like "not with the head only, but also with the heart." The head then represents the intellect, and the heart is where the emotions and feelings have their say. Yet in one of those meditations Kuyper says explicitly, "*Mind you, I am not talking now about the heart as the organ of your emotions but as that point within you where God works and from where He works on your head as well as your brain—that point in your existence where life is still undivided.*"[91] And then he uses

---

[91] What Dooyeweerd here quotes from memory is not found in *Op den Pinksterdag*. The first part of the sentence occurs in *Honig uit den Rotssteen*, 2 vols. (Amsterdam, 1880, 1883), II, 35 (2nd impr., p. 26); cf. p. 372 in the Eng. trans. by James A. De Jong (see n. 65). The closing part, with the clause "where life is still undivided" is found in Kuyper's *Lectures on Calvinism* (1898; Grand Rapids, MI: Eerdmans, 1931), p. 20: the heart is "that point in our consciousness in which our life is still undivided and lies comprehended in its unity..." The lecture continues: "Personally it is our repeated experience that in the depths of our hearts, at the point where we

the example of the root and the many stems and branches that come up from the root: "not in the spreading vines," he says, "but in the very root of our being."[92] That is the pregnant sense in which the Bible talks about the heart.

Well, I can say that this discovery was a turning point in my life. When I began to dwell on this idea, I realized that this insight would mean a complete overturning of my view of man and the whole of reality in which we live, for that reality has really found its concentration in man alone ... in his "selfhood" as the centre in which all our temporal capacities and all our temporal functions are concentrated, whether it be thinking, feeling, organic life, and what not, all focused on the centre, on the 'I' as their centre: I believe, I think, I feel, I live, and so on. All these functions of living, thinking, believing, feeling, etc.—all these come to a focus and are concentrically related to the human 'I' as the centre, indeed as the religious centre.

The biblical view of the human heart would become a keynote in the years that followed, as Dooyeweerd worked out his ontology and epistemology (and to a small extent his anthropology) in a full-fledged philosophical system which he called

---

disclose ourselves to the Eternal One, *all the rays of our life converge as in one focus*, and there alone regain that harmony which we so often and so painfully lose in the stress of daily duty" (emph. added). Evidently, Dooyeweerd conflated several passages from different works by Kuyper.

[92] The original reads: "not in the spreading vines but in the root from which the vines spring." *Lectures on Calvinism*, p. 20.

II. Kuyper's Heirs 73

De Wijsbegeerte der Wetsidee,[93] and in its revised and expanded version, *The Philosophy of the Cosmonomic Idea*.[94]

And so was fulfilled a long-standing wish, often voiced by Kuyper himself: that the Neo-Calvinist movement might be equipped with a philosophy of its own, developed from a disciplined study of God's Word and God's works. It was a capstone achievement building on the legacy of Abraham Kuyper.

Summary

Our selection of seven heirs of Kuyper illustrates that each in his own way contributed to the legacy we can look at today: relating to developing nations as a sacred trust and a challenge for gospel missions; defending a plural education system that honors parental rights; adopting an uncompromising stance toward tyranny of every sort; and struggling to practice an integral Christian approach to the discipline of philosophy and to scholarship in general.

It is up to present-day researchers of Neo-Calvinism to mine this legacy for all it's worth; to weed out what is dated and what was misguided; to inspire a new generation to stand in the breach against the onslaughts of secularism, and in a spirit of compassion and humility to offer biblical alternatives for the healing of the societies in which they have been placed.

---

[93] H. Dooyeweerd, *De Wijsbegeerte der Wetsidee*, 3 vols. (Amsterdam: H. J. Paris Uitgeverij, 1935–36).

[94] H. Dooyeweerd, *A New Critique of Theoretical Thought*, 4 vols. (Philadelphia: Presb. and Reformed Pub. Co., 1953–58).

III. SOME LESSONS FROM THIS HISTORY

We have traversed almost a century and a half to get a sense of one particular witness to the liberating gospel of Jesus Christ. What can be learned from our journey? Here follow some points for discussion.[95]

1. Groen van Prinsterer's early identification of the Enlightenment project—"the Revolution"—as the root of modernity, with its cultural ramifications everywhere, put his small group spiritually on guard against the secularization of culture and forced it to think up alternative responses as the various challenges of modernization presented themselves: participatory government, universal public education, the social question resulting from industrialization and urbanization, the new media of newsprint and public broadcast.[96]

---

[95] As explained in the Preface, Part III, as well as Part IV, was added in the interest of the theme chosen for the consultation in 1996 with Lesslie Newbiggin, namely: "Kuyperianism and the Public Square: A Tradition of Christian Cultural Engagement."

[96] The contest over radio frequencies, broadcast time and program requirements is analyzed in John L. Hiemstra, *The Role of Worldviews in the Politics of Accommodation: A Case Study of Dutch Broadcasting Policy, 1919–1930* (Ph.D. thesis; University of Calgary, 1993). This well-documented study shows that the medium of radio and the airways in general became the monopoly neither of the government nor of religiously neutral organizations nor yet of profit-

2. The liberals who took control after 1848 envisioned a public order borne up by an "enlightened" form of Protestantism transcending "sectarian" differences. This vision was challenged from the start. Neither Catholics nor Protestants were willing to be reduced to private sects. But for their resistance, Holland would fast have become a homogeneous secular society.[97]

3. The very hostility of secular liberalism in Holland forced orthodox Christians to see themselves as "a party," not as "the nation." This situation fostered the formation of separate Christian organizations as the most effective way of entering the fray to contend for shaping the public order.[98]

---

oriented business ventures, but was proportionally distributed over worldview-tinted ("ideological") organizations supported by dues-paying members. Once this mutual accommodation was achieved, the same pattern was followed when television made its debut—the natural outcome of the system of consociational democracy.

[97] This thesis is defended by Stanley Carlson-Thies in his "The Role of Protestants and Catholics in the Development of Dutch Politics in the 19th and 20th Centuries" (diss., Univ. of Toronto, 1994).

[98] J. Klapwijk distinguishes eight motives which, singly or in combination, account for the rise of separate Christian organizations in the Netherlands: 1) frustration: distress about existing impediments to effective Christian witness; 2) *pro Rege*: crusading on behalf of the kingship of Christ over all of life; 3) patrimony: to safeguard or recover the national Christian heritage; 4) rechristianization: to transform people and reform society; 5) antithesis: demarcating the line separating believers from unbelievers, contrasting Christian thought with humanist thinking, etc.; 6) principles: underscoring one's distinctive approach to problems and

III. Some Lessons from This History

4. It was in part their failure to reform the national church that encouraged the men of Groen and Kuyper's generations to throw more of their energy into non-ecclesiastical action, asserting a multi-faceted Christian presence in Dutch society at large.

5. A visible Christian presence in Dutch society was not in the first place the triumph of a repressed minority vying for power. It was the almost unintended result of a few Christian men of influence who acknowledged the responsibilities of their office. The pioneers of anti-revolutionary politics—Groen, Elout, Mackay—each brought Christian norms to bear on the task they faced in public life—on their *office* as a Member of Parliament, as a Justice in a provincial court, and as a Councillor of State respectively. The same can be said of orthodox believers who realized their office as parents by founding independent schools to provide their children with a Christian education; of pastors like Heldring and Talma who fulfilled their office by ministering their flocks with the mercies of Christ; and of Kater who witnessed in "neutral" labour unions and as a result was forced to devote his energies to a separate labour movement.

---

thereby vindicating its right to vie with other approaches; 7) coming-of-age: the awakening of the common man, the assertion of the freedom of the layman; 8) emancipation: to undo discrimination of the orthodox and ensure equal rights for all, not as an end in itself but as a means toward realizing stated ideals. See Jacob Klapwijk, "Christelijke organisaties in verlegenheid," in *Christelijke organisaties in discussie; een bijdrage*, published by the Vereniging van Christelijke Studenten te Amsterdam (The Hague: Boekencentrum, 1979), 21–66.

6. This tradition exhibited a passion for reordering society, for structural ("architectonic") critique. It focused as much on tackling the disease as on relieving the symptoms. Although such a focus at times can be in tension with an emphasis on providing the so-called band-aid solutions of Christian mercy, the Neo-Calvinist, Kuyperian tradition—fortunately for the victims and the weak, the vulnerable, and the helpless—stimulated not one but both forms of witness (see Part IV below).

7. The case study of the Netherlands shows what to avoid:

(a) equating an action program with the Kingdom of God: annexing God for one's human (and therefore finite and fallible) cause. If the identification is too close, Christian action programs can bring the Christian gospel itself into disrepute whenever the shortcomings or failures of Christian programs become apparent.

(b) relying on power, former glory, strategy, group-think (tribalism), and leadership (the cult of personality. This worldliness was much in evidence around Kuyper and the five-time anti-revolutionary prime minister Hendrikus Colijn.[99]

(c) using impure arguments, especially in the early stages, by standing on guard for the "national heritage" and claiming historically acquired (and lost) rights. This emphasis weakened the claims of divinely ordained rights, freedoms, and obligations.

---

[99] Cf. Ben van Kaam, *Parade der mannenbroeders: Flitsen uit het protestantse leven in Nederland in de jaren 1918–1938* (Wageningen: Zomer & Keuning, 1964). The author made no claim to be offering a scholarly study of the phenomenon of self-satisfied Kuyperians publicly parading in triumph; he styled his book "a journalistic exploration of contemporary newspapers, magazines, pamphlets and personal diaries."

III. Some Lessons from This History

(d) developing smugness, a sense of having arrived after initial gains. This attitude undermined Christian humility, sapped reforming zeal, and led to uncritical conservatism, evident especially during the interbellum (1920–40). Cf. n. 99 above.

8. Our case study also suggests what to emulate:

(a) dedication of Christians to the public cause, no withdrawal from practical affairs for whatever reason (fear, disdain, the dualism of world-flight);

(b) a transfer of the fight to the opposition's battleground, rather than criticism from the safe confines of the church; the list must be entered where anti-Christian forces are the strongest: today that would be the media and the universities, elsewhere perhaps public corruption and oppressive economic structures;

(c) the adoption of a principled pluralism that fights the spiritual warfare with weapons of persuasion, not coercion;

(d) the development of a well-rounded worldview which assigns worship, moral living etc. their crucial yet relative place in living the full Christian life and which emphasizes the cosmic scope of Christ's redemptive work, affording indestructible hope and restoring confidence in the creation order which, though soiled and spoiled by sin, yet remains intact as the universally valid framework in which human life is meant to flourish;

(e) resisting an exclusive concentration on a burning issue of the day and instead, after clearly identifying the common cause of public malaise, working painstakingly at developing viable alternatives for the whole range of cultural sectors;

(f) respect for all human callings, personal initiatives, grassroots knowledge, local experience, instead of centralized control, ivory-tower blueprints, organizational strait-jackets; and in the same vein: to observe sphere sovereignty (differentiated responsibility, diversity of offices).

9. A final lesson, particularly apt for Anglo-phone countries: however useful and valuable they are, we are not to rely and build on a Christian *denomination* to lead a Christian society,[100] nor on a Christian *theology* to guide the Christian mind.[101] These may assist and support, but leadership must come from informed and engaged laymen vocationally active in the various fields and disciplines.

---

[100] See, e.g., T. S. Eliot, *The Idea of a Christian Society* (London: Faber, 1939).

[101] See, e.g., H. Blamires, *The Christian Mind* (London: S.P.C.K., 1963).

IV. SOME PROTESTANT PILLARS

In a modest booklet of just under a hundred pages, published in 1938 by the Central Federation for Inner Mission and Christian Philanthropic Institutions under the title *Veertig Jaar Christelijk Maatschappelijke Arbeid in Nederland*, we learn of an interesting variety of Protestant social work during the first forty years of the reign of Queen Wilhelmina, 1898–1938. (I do not know of a similar publication from the Roman Catholic side.)

In the introduction, A. de Graaf, president of the federation, notes that the period was marked by important legislation such as Childcare Laws, the Acts for the Care of Psychopaths, regulations for conditional sentences, probation and rehabilitation, and anti-prostitution laws, all of which came about with the help of the Christian political parties. De Graaf explains that a knowledgeable person from each area of social work has been asked to contribute a succinct report to the booklet outlining that work and the organizational network that is engaged in it.

The first chapter reports on care for the unemployed, still very much needed in 1938. Following an international congress in Basel in 1932, a Council of Netherlands Churches for Practical Christianity was established. Besides operating nine work camps throughout the country, those engaged in this work also run many training and recreation camps as well as Bible study courses.

Next, we read about homes for armed forces personnel. There are 27 such centres, located near army camps and naval bases. Here, enlisted men can relax, read, sing, hear the Christian message, and be counselled during off-duty hours. Closely related are several societies for the propagation of the gospel among officers and non-commissioned officers.

An Association of Friends of Young Women busies itself with job mediation via placement bureaus and operating clubs and shelters in urban centres and information booths at major railway stations.

In the next chapter, a score of group homes are listed, including four owned by the Salvation Army, which offer aid to unwed mothers and ex-prostitutes. There are 9 affiliated associations in this area of work, which goes back to turn-of-the-century moral campaigns inspired by Josephine Butler and the first Immorality Act passed by the Dutch parliament in 1911. There is also a National Committee against Pornography and Traffic in Women and Children.

A list of 36 organizations highlights the work being done for the care of Crown wards, foundlings, foster children, juvenile delinquents, neglected infants and abused minors. Their stated aim is to make their charges "socially useful human beings and, if possible, followers of Jesus Christ." Privately financed for centuries, the work has enjoyed some government subsidies since 1901.

In the next chapter it is Professor Herman Dooyeweerd of the Law Faculty in the Free University at Amsterdam who reports on organizations devoted to the work of rehabilitation. This work too had seen a transition from strictly private to partially public funding, effective as of 1910. Under the probation system, he explains, there is ongoing need for more

IV. Some Protestant Pillars

help to those on suspended sentences. The work involved many volunteers and included prison visitation, job placement, and the operating of asylums for vagrants and alcoholics.

The reader then hears about a dozen temperance unions and societies for teetotalism, established at the turn of the century. They run homes, organize conferences, publish a monthly, and work the media.

Next, there is the work of care for the poor and slum dwellers. With the growth of social welfare programs, we learn, church diaconates now concentrate on the moral and spiritual dimensions of the problem of poverty. Care for the aged gets a chapter by itself: it reports on Protestant rest homes, nursing homes, and other types of long-term care facilities. Related work is done by Protestant hospitals—no fewer than 37 are listed—and a national organization for home nursing and health education. A felt need for sanatoria with a positive Christian atmosphere resulted in 1905, and again in 1927, in the founding of a separate Protestant institution for sufferers of tuberculosis. Cures are expensive, it is reported, but fund drives help defray the costs.

Compassionate care for epileptics, one of the earliest forms of Christian philanthropy in modern Holland, is represented by three institutions for observation and treatment, the most prominent one being "Meer en Bosch" near Harlem. The early start, at a time when safety and comfort but no effective relief (let alone a cure) was possible, enabled these institutions to be at the forefront of new developments with the advancement of medical knowledge and techniques. In 1938 the umbrella organization also operated three consulting clinics in different cities.

Professor Jan Waterink, head of the Institute for Child Psychology affiliated with the Free University in Amsterdam, reports on the various institutions for care of the mentally retarded and the mentally ill. In addition to listing the main asylums, the first of which dates from 1890, Waterink mentions in particular the many Protestant schools for special education for mentally challenged children as well as the growing number of sheltered workplaces.

New hope dawned in the 19th century for neuropaths and psychopaths when shackles and straitjackets were replaced by recreation and occupational therapy, and maids and orderlies made way for specialized trained nurses. Starting in 1884, Christian psychiatric hospitals grew to a number of 10 by 1938.

Attention is paid next to homes for physically disabled children and to residential schools for the deaf and for the blind. There are also reports on summer outdoor camps for inner city children and "health colonies" that provide vacation weeks for weak, undernourished, or convalescent children.

The booklet closes with a chapter on training schools for Christian social workers. Equally significant, this description is followed by a list of eight national federations (the oldest dating from 1899) that functioned as umbrella organizations in which Protestant associations collaborated with their Catholic, Jewish, and "neutral" counterparts.

Impressive though the achievements enumerated in this booklet may be for a small country of at that time 8 million inhabitants, similar records could be compiled for countries like Austria, Switzerland, Germany, the United Kingdom, and elsewhere. Even in the jurisdiction where I live, the Canadian

IV. Some Protestant Pillars

province of Ontario, we have a few pillars.[102] The point to note about the Netherlands is that as the welfare state grew apace after 1945, most of these organizations—belonging to whatever "directional" or 'ideological" type, religious or otherwise—were treated on a parity basis in respect of accreditation and government subsidies. This hallmark of "accommodation politics"—more accurately named "institutionalized worldview pluralism"—is one of the enduring legacies of the culture wars in which Abraham Kuyper played such a dominant role.

---

[102] For example, Ontario has *public* schools (originally Protestant, now religiously "neutral") and *separate* schools (Roman Catholic), both publicly financed; it sponsors a Children's Aid Society and a Catholic Children's Aid Society; the province boasts, next to many General Hospitals, a St. Luke's Hospital, a St. Joseph's Hospital, and a Mount Sinai Hospital.

INDEX OF NAMES

Aldegonde, *see* Marnix
Alphen, H. van — 1

Bavinck, H. — 1, 4
Beeremans, W. C. — 31-33
Beets, N. — 15
Beza, Th. — 41
Bilderdijk, W. — 1-6, 8, 10
Bishop, Steve — viii
Bismarck, Otto von — 51
Blamires, H. — 80
Bornebroek, A. — 58
Bosch, J. — 4
Brinkel, B. F. M. — 51
Brock, Cory C. — 6
Bratt, James D. — 42
Bruijn, J. de — 49, 51
Burke, Edmund — 10, 41
Butler, Josephine — 82

Calvin, J. — 41
Capadose, A. — 7
Carlson-Thies, S. — 76
Colijn, H. — 48, 78
Costa, Isaac da — 7-10, 24, 40

De Jong, James A. — 49, 72
Delleman, Th. — 67
Dooyeweerd, H. — 11, 68, 70-73, 82

Eijnatten, J. van — 5
Eliot, T. S. — 80

Elout van Soeterwoude, P. J. — 14f, 15, 23, 77
Engelen, Ph. — 70
Essen, J. L. van — 14
Esser, I. — 24-27

Fogarty, M. — 34

Geer van Jutphaas, B. J. L. de — 16
Gerretson, C. — 48
Gladstone, W. E. — 47
Goheen, M. — ix
Graaf, A. de — 81
Groen van Prinsterer, G. — 9, 10-19, 24, 25, 30, 33, 35, 36f, 41, 42, 43, 69, 75, 77
Guizot, F. — 41

Hagoort, R. — 28f, 35f, 38
Hansen, D. — ix
Hasebroek, J. P. — 7, 15, 40
Heemskerk, Th. — 61
Heldring, O. G. — 19-21, 77
Hiemstra, J. L. — 75
Hitler, A. — 65
Hoop, L. de — 58
Hotman, F. — 41

Idenburg, A. — 53-57

Jong, L. de — 67

Kaam, Ben van — 78
Kater, K. — 27-38, 77
Keuchenius, L. W. Chr. — 50-53

Kingsley, Ch.	58	Romein-Verschoor, A.	48
Klapwijk, J.	76f	Rullmann, J. C.	9
Kluit, M. E.	8	Rutgers, V. H.	66–70
Kok, J. H.	viii	Schouten, J.	64–66
Kooi, C. van der	49	Schutte, G. J.	51
Kossmann, E. H.	60	Skillen, J. W.	39
Kuipers, Tj.	50	Smeenk, C.	60
Kuyper, A.	27, 33, 39–48, 62; *et passim*	Smid, T.	25
		Smitskamp, H.	17
Langley, McKendree	47, 61	Snel, Johan	50
Languet, H.	41	Stahl, F. J.	41
Liefde, J. L. de	9	Stalin, J.	65
Lijphart, A.	34	Strauss, D. F. M.	3
Lloyd-Jones, D. Martyn	12	Sutanto, N. Gray	6
Lohman, A. F. de Savornin	63–64	Talma, S.	57–63, 77
		Tocqueville, A. de	12
Mackay Jr., A.	38	Troelstra, P. J.	60
Mackay Sr. A.	14, 77	VanderStelt, J. C.	ix
Malsen, H. van	59	VanderVelde, G.	ix
Marnix van St. Aldegonde, Philips	41	Van Meggelen, J.	70
Marx, K.	30	Vellinga, J. M.	58, 63
Maurice, F. D.	58	Voetius, G.	41
Miller, E.	23	Wagenman, M.	49
Newbiggin, L.	ix, 75, 95	Waterink, J.	84
Newcastle, Eustace Percy of	59	Wehring, J. van	25
Nieuwenhuis, Domela	60	Werkman, Paul E.	28
Nijhoff, Rob	34	Westerhuis, D. J. A.	8
Overduin, J.	68	Wilde, J. A. de	60
Pater, J. C. H. de	68	Witmond, J.	32, 33
Postma, A.	51	Wolbers, J.	28–30
Proudhon, P. J.	37	Wormser, J. A.	21–24
Puchinger, G.	48	Zythoff, Gerrit J. ten	8
Reest, Rudolf van	6		

INDEX OF SUBJECTS

Abolition Society 23
Achin 52, 55
alcoholism 60
Anti-Revolutionary Party 38, 47, 49, 50, 58, 66, 69
Anti-School Law League 47

Calvinism viii, 41
capitalism 52
Christian Labour Association of Canada vii
Christian Social Congress 39, 58
Christian Socialists 58, 59
Church and State 14, 22f, 47, 58, 80
class struggle 31, 37
communism 64f
compulsory cultivation 52, 57
concubinage 57
conservatism 44, 79

East Indies 24f, 50–57
Enlightenment 11, 75
ethical colonial policy 52, 57

fascism 65, 66
free enterprise 52, 62
Free University 25
French Revolution 8, 11, 26, 29, 58
grass roots 27, 80

Grievances Against the Spirit of the Age 7
heart, concept of 70–72
Heraut, De 27
Hinduism 56

imperialism 54
Indonesia, *see* East Indies
International, the 29f, 32
Islam 52, 56
Isolationism 16

Labour Code 47
liberalism 12, 45, 76
 -Christian 45
 -economic 57

missions 52, 55, 56
 -inner mission 60, 81
modernism, theological 18, 21

national socialism 65–69
Nederlandsche Gedachten 41, 42
Neo-Calvinism viii, 5, 13, 34, 73, 78

office, concept of 77
opium 57
Orange, House of 2, 56

pacifism 66
people
 -"the little" 2
 -"behind the voters" 17, 27

Patrimonium	33–38, 58		41f, 47, 69
People's Petition	47	Stone Lectures	vii
permanent revolution	12	suffrage	17, 64
pillarization	24, 81–85	Sumatra	52
pluralism	47, 63f, 79	Sunday observance	32, 57, 62
prostitution	60	Suriname	54, 56
railway strikes	61	theology, place of	80
religion	11	ultramontanism	44
Réveil	7, 19	*Unbelief and Revolution*	11–16,
Restoration, the	12		25, 65, 69
Revolution, the	12, 13, 22,	universities	46
	25, 38, 45		
schools struggle	18f, 33, 57,	*Werkmansvriend, De*	28–32,
	63f, 67f		35, 38
secularization	56, 75	Westerbork Camp	68
self-help	29, 63	Whiggism	2
Social Insurance	62	White Man's Burden	54
socialism	62, 66	world flight	79
sphere sovereignty	62, 80	World War I	62
Standaard, De	16, 27, 33,	World War II	66